YOUR
MANUFACTURING
COMPANY

ABOUT THE AUTHOR

Robert A. Crinkley is the northwest associate of Management Partners, a professional management firm. Mr. Crinkley's consulting activity with Management Partners covers high-technology products and markets. His clients include manufacturers of electronic, electromechanical, mechanical, and chemical processing products ranging in size from a start-up cadre of three entrepreneurs to a completely integrated operation of over one thousand people.

Mr. Crinkley also serves the business community of San Juan County, Washington, as the coordinator and instructor for a small business management adult educational program sponsored by Skagit Valley College of Mount Vernon, Washington.

He is an active member of the board of directors of several of his client companies and lives near the village of Eastsound on Orcas Island.

YOUR MANUFACTURING COMPANY

How to Start It / How to Manage It

ROBERT A. CRINKLEY

Northwest Associate
Management Partners
A Professional Management Firm

Coordinator, Instructor
Small Business Management
Skagit Valley College

McGRAW-HILL BOOK COMPANY

*New York   St. Louis   San Francisco   Auckland   Bogotá   Hamburg
Johannesburg   London   Madrid   Mexico   Montreal   New Delhi   Panama
Paris   São Paulo   Singapore   Sydney   Tokyo   Toronto*

Library of Congress Cataloging in Publication Data

Crinkley, Robert A.
  Your manufacturing company.

  Includes index.
  1. New business enterprises—Management.
  2. Industrial management. 3. Production management.
  I. Title.
  HD62.5.C74   658   81-20801
  ISBN 0-07-013680-7   AACR2

1 2 3 4 5 6 7 8 9 0   DODO   8 9 8 7 6 5 4 3 2

ISBN 0-07-013680-7

The editors for this book were William Newton and Alice
Manning, the designer was Elliot Epstein, and the production
supervisor was Thomas G. Kowalczyk. It was set in Century
Schoolbook by University Graphics, Inc.

Printed and bound by R. R. Donnelley & Sons Company.

CONTENTS

v

PREFACE

Your Manufacturing Company is the first text to provide everything needed to organize and manage the day-to-day operations of a manufacturing company.

The start-up company entrepreneur can use the book as an operating manual to get the business launched and underway in a matter of hours or, at the most, days.

Ongoing company entrepreneurs and functional executives will find the book an excellent guide for refining or streamlining business systems as their operations expand and become more complex.

The student contemplating a career in the manufacturing sector will find the book to be a synopsis of the many texts that provide in-depth treatment of individual manufacturing-company functions. It ties all the functions together to provide an integrated overview of operating and managing a manufacturing company.

Most currently available texts related to manufacturing companies cover a single function in more depth and detail than the working entrepreneur, functional executive, or student really needs or can assimilate. These texts are also oriented to large, sophisticated, and highly structured organizations rather than small businesses. They are long on theory and woefully short on application of the theories in solving day-to-day operating problems. *Your Manufacturing Company* contains real-world functional business systems that can be put into practice quickly and easily to produce immediate results. The book is seasoned with strategies, tactics, and techniques that are problem solvers or have enhanced the success of others.

This book is a compendium of over forty functional business systems needed to organize and manage the day-to-day operations of a manufacturing company. Each system is succinctly yet thoroughly described and discussed. The language peculiar to each function is explained. Inputs to each system, the system process, the output of the system, and how systems interact are covered. Step-by-step flowcharts accompanied by a narrative discussion of the what, why, who, and when of each action step or transaction are provided. Suggested first-cut management policies, decision rules, and approval limits are included.

The systems covered in this book are not new or theoretical concepts—they are time-honored, proven systems that have evolved and been refined over time into industry norms. The same or close variations of these systems are in daily use in countless successful manufacturing companies.

Finally, the thrust of this book is to save the entrepreneur precious hours and days in establishing the functional business systems needed to operate and manage the company. Those precious hours and days are better spent in developing the product line and getting it to the marketplace.

Robert A. Crinkley

PART ONE
INTRODUCTION

The two chapters in Part 1—"About the Book" and "The Manufacturing-Company Language"—set the stage and provide the background, assumptions, and premises underlying the manufacturing-company functional business systems covered in this book.

CHAPTER 1: ABOUT THE BOOK

This chapter describes the resource base that underpins the total enterprise and the allocation of that resource base to the functions that perform the day-to-day operations of the business. It describes and discusses the major manufacturing-company functions: what they do and how they meld into the total operation; it also describes the composition of the functional business systems that coordinate, control, and manage the company. It also explains how to use the book to construct and implement functional business systems in start-up and ongoing manufacturing companies.

CHAPTER 2: THE MANUFACTURING-COMPANY LANGUAGE

This chapter contains a discussion of the language unique to manufacturing companies that integrates the many manufacturing-company functions into a contiguous whole. It defines and interprets what the language means to and the effect it has on the operation and management of the business.

1

ABOUT
THE BOOK

All manufacturing companies require a set of resources that underpin the total enterprise: a product line that fits the marketplace, physical facilities, equipment, money, people, and management. A major initial task of the start-up manufacturing-company entrepreneur is to provide this resource base. It must be sufficient to launch and sustain the enterprise until it has become self-supporting. A significant continuing task of the ongoing manufacturing-company entrepreneur is to modulate and expand the resource base to support the changing needs of the enterprise as it evolves and expands.

RESOURCE BASE ELEMENTS

This book starts with the premise that the resource base is in place and treats the task of allocating resources to, and managing, the many manufacturing-company functions that perform the day-to-day operations of the business. First, it gives a brief discussion of the elements of the resource base.

Product Line, Marketplace

Start-up manufacturing companies usually commence operations with a single product or a limited product line that the owners and financial backers feel will meet the projections in the business plan. By definition, successful ongoing manufacturing companies have a product line that fits the marketplace. Keeping the product line viable and growing is a key requisite for success. The product selection process includes a determination of which products should remain in the line, which should be phased out, and, importantly, how to decide which new products to develop and add to the line.

Facilities

Start-up manufacturing companies often commence operation in the garage or basement workshop of one of the partners. As the business evolves from a start-up to an ongoing situation, a rented or leased facility makes sense. The type of facility and its location are functions of the manufacturing process and the availability of vacant space. Cost and flexibility—the ability to easily and rapidly expand or contract—are key facility decision factors.

Equipment

The equipment required to develop and manufacture the product can be purchased or leased. It is often possible to subcontract operations that require expensive specialized equipment. The decision to purchase, lease, or subcontract is dependent first on availability of cash and second on the rate of return on investment to purchase or lease versus the cost to subcontract.

People

Quite often the start-up company cadre is yourself, possibly your spouse, and one or more partners. Of necessity, all the business functions must be performed by the initial cadre. As the business expands, the "all things by all people" configuration will evolve into functional departments supervised or managed by trained and experienced functional executives.

Financing

A comprehensive, well-prepared business plan is almost always required to secure initial or first-round financing from outside sources. It is recommended that the business plan be revised or upgraded annually. A primary reason for the annual business-plan update is to disclose requirements for additional growth, working, or equity capital well in advance of actual need so that subsequent rounds of financing can be planned and secured on the most favorable terms.

Management

People who manage manufacturing companies have learned that the seeming maze of parts, material, equipment, facilities, money, and people must be controlled and coordinated to provide order and continuity in the day-to-day operation of the business. Successful manufacturing companies provide control, coordination, and continuity through functional business systems of interlocking data and information flow—forms and reports—gathered manually, mechanically, or electronically. This book will show you how to construct such systems for your company.

Manufacturing-Company Functions

A common denominator of all manufacturing companies, regardless of the product line, is a need to cope with a relatively large population of sizes, shapes, and types of purchased material, in-house fabricated parts, and purchased parts. A manufacturer of blue jeans must cope with legs, pockets, waistbands, and belt loops fabricated in many sizes and styles from material of different colors and weights, together with purchased buttons, zippers, and the all-important rear pocket brand label. Kitchen cupboard manufacturers are involved with different styles and sizes of doors, drawers, sides, tops, bottoms, back panels, and shelves, fabricated from different types of wood, and with purchased items such as hinges, screws, drawer slides, door pulls, nails, glue, and finishing materials. A manufacturer of computer products handles a myriad of electronic components, circuit cards, wire, enclosures, hardware, and so on.

The coping mechanism is to organize the company into functions so that each function performs a discrete and defined portion of the day-to-day operation of the business.

Marketing   The marketing function is the conduit between the company and the marketplace. Inputs from the marketplace to the company influence the specifications for new products, indicate the demand for existing products, and provide feedback on the activity of the competition. Activity from the company to the marketplace produces orders.

Product Development The product development function designs new products and provides the manufacturing functions with the documentation and technical support that enable the product to be produced.

Post-Sale Support The post-sale support function provides the services necessary to install the product, train the customer to use the product, and maintain the product.

Material Requirements Planning The material requirements planning function determines how many of which items are needed on what date to support manufacturing the product in accordance with a master schedule.

Purchasing The purchasing function procures from outside sources all goods and services needed to operate the business.

Work in Process The work in process function consists of planning for and providing sufficient work force, space, and equipment to enable manufactured parts and assemblies to be completed in accordance with the master schedule.

Receiving The receiving function receives all goods or commodities purchased from outside sources. It assures that what is received is the correct quantity of what was ordered and that it is not damaged.

Stockroom The stockroom function stores, controls, protects from damage, and issues parts and materials to the manufacturing process.

Shipping The shipping function packages, packs, and arranges for shipment of all products or commodities shipped by the company.

Quality Control The quality control function inspects and tests all purchased parts and material, work in process, and finished goods to assure compliance with established company quality and reliability criteria.

Accounting   The accounting function maintains the company accounting system: journals, ledgers, and financial statements. Accounting also handles all financial transactions: accounts payable, accounts receivable, payroll, debit and credit memos, and others.

Cost   The cost function allocates all costs incurred by the company to the proper account and provides management with an analysis of the variance between planned or standard cost and actual cost.

Cash Management   Cash management is a management function that involves planning and securing the financing required to underwrite the operation and controlling cash flow in accordance with the plan.

Functional Business Systems

In its simplest form, managing or running a manufacturing company is a never-ending series of decisions and implementation of decisions. In a start-up situation, the entrepreneur makes and implements all the decisions. As the business grows and expands, more and more people become involved in decision making and implementation. To control the business as it grows and expands, the entrepreneur establishes functional business systems consisting of decision rules, paperwork, a process, and people.

Decision Rules   Decision rules are management policies that govern or confine decisions made by individual functions within predetermined parameters, for example, how much inventory to buy and carry, what types of parts are to be covered by an engineering drawing, when sales commissions are to be paid, what types of purchases require quotations, and the mark-up ratio for pricing spare parts.

Paperwork   Paperwork consists of forms and the data entered on them that either cause or are the result of an action step taken by someone, that record transactions, that are running or perpetual records, or that are planning documents or "to do" lists. A *purchase order* form is the paperwork that starts a procurement transaction. The *vendor invoice* and *packing list* are the paperwork that completes a procurement transaction. Paperwork can be a physical piece of paper, or it can take the form of a video terminal display of the same data.

Process In the context of a functional business system, the process is the procedure or sequential steps the paperwork follows as it moves through the organization to complete an action or transaction. The process of a procurement transaction, for example, starts with a requirement to purchase something, recorded on a purchase order form. Typical steps in the purchasing process include receiving approval, securing quotations, negotiating terms, issuing the purchase order, and following up to assure delivery. Ancillary steps of this process include recording the open order on the on-order record and possibly on a short sheet. Receipt of what was ordered triggers the receiving process: inspecting for damage, identification, count or quantity verification, and creation of the receiving ticket. Copies of the receiving ticket cause the receipt to be posted to the on-order record, short sheet, and inventory record and also trigger the accounts payable process: matching the certified-count receiving ticket and vendor packing list with the vendor invoice, and issuing payment to the vendor. The payment transaction triggers the cost process of posting the cost history record, debiting stockroom inventory, crediting cash, and debiting or crediting variance.

People People make it all happen: they make decisions, create documents, calculate, post, and move the paperwork through the process. Functional business systems in the form of operating manuals provide them with decision rules, examples of the forms they use, flowcharts, and instructions that they need to perform their job and tell them where the paperwork comes from, what they are to do, how they are to do it, why they do it, and where the paperwork goes when they have completed their task.

ABOUT THE BOOK

This book describes over forty functional business systems in sixteen chapters that are organized in six parts.

Part One: Introduction

Part 1 includes this chapter and a discussion of the unique language of manufacturing companies.

Part Two: The Product Line, The Marketplace

Part 2 discusses the functions that interface with, influence, or are influenced by the marketplace.

Part Three: The Start-Up Manufacturing System

Part 3 explains the bare-bones system needed in start-up or small ongoing companies.

Part Four: The Larger Ongoing Company Manufacturing System

Part 4 explains the more sophisticated systems needed as the company expands and grows.

Part Five: Financial Control Systems

Part 5 discusses systems not directly involved in day-to-day operations that provide internal control of the financial side of the business.

Part Six: Documentation

Part 6 is a catalog of forms.

If you are in the throes of launching a start-up company, concentrate on Parts 1, 2, and 3 and ignore Part 4. Skimming Part 5 should provide some ideas or concepts that will help your launching exercise. Everything except Part 3 should be of use to larger ongoing companies.

In any case, you will find that the description and discussion of each functional business system will provide you with:

- A basic flowchart, if needed, to follow the more complex systems, which can serve as a model for developing your own

- Illustrations and explanations of the basic data-gathering and reporting documents needed

- Advice about exercising control over the function

- Suggestions about which forms to use when starting a company, which ones to use in more advanced operations, and which are optional

Start-Up Systems

The minimum systems needed to support a start-up situation are suggested. Some companies may need more than those suggested, some may need less. Precisely what is needed in each specific start-up situation is a judgment call. Much more than the minimum is probably not necessary; much less may cause problems.

Ongoing Systems

The minimum systems invoked in a start-up situation are often adequate to support a small ongoing situation. It is recommended that you not expand a system that is adequately supporting a given function just because the company has grown and other systems are expanding and becoming more sophisticated. System expansion means adding database documents, working documents, and copies of documents. Adding documents and copies means adding people to create, process, and file them. It is better to err by not allowing system expansion than to expand systems in anticipation of an assumed need. Once documents or copies become entrenched in the system, they are practically impossible to withdraw.

Computer-Based Systems

Most successful manufacturing companies eventually reach a size that warrants conversion from manual to computer-based systems. Successful computer-based systems are almost always preceded by successful manual systems.

All the systems in this book are described and discussed in terms of manual operation. All of them are readily convertible to existing computer-based systems. Computer-based systems consist of a database called the product information file; buffers, which are suspense files or buckets for temporary storage of data; memory or permanent history files of data; and programs or routines, which are processes to perform the tasks of functional business systems.

The product information file is the heart of a computer-based system. It is a combination of permanent data and working data. Data are filed in the product information file by part number. Each part number file contains all the data that pertain to that part number: bill of material, used-on, vendor data, on-order, on-hand, shortages, standard cost, stockroom location, and any other data.

The *permanent data* include data that are permanent or subject to very infrequent change. When you convert your manual system to a computer-based system, most of the data on your manual system database documents will be entered into the product information file.

The level or quantity of working data contained in the product information file is dependent on the design or framework of the computer-based system. How it is entered into the computer and how it is read out are also a function of the specific computer system. Data may be keyed in via a terminal or entered via punched cards, punched paper tape, or magnetic tape. Data readout can be via a video display terminal, a paper printout, or both.

The extent of data processing done by the computer and by humans also varies among systems. Some systems will print out completely cut work orders, purchase orders, and vendor reschedule letters. Other systems will print out action notices that require manual preparation of work orders and purchase orders.

The accounts payable and purchased parts and material cost accounting processes provide a good illustration of manual versus computer data processing.

The manual systems are described in Chapters 12 and 13. Purchased parts and material cost accounting is depicted in Figure 13-5. The manual process consists of account distribution; posting the standard cost debit to stockroon inventory; posting freight in, taxes, and other such charges to expense accounts; posting the credit to accounts payable; calculating variance and posting it to variance accounts; filing and retrieving the payable from the suspense file; posting the debit to accounts payable; posting the credit to cash; and typing the vendor check.

In a typical computer-based system, a vendor number, invoice data, and a payment date are entered into the computer. The computer will access the product information file and vendor memory file and will debit standard cost to stockroom inventory; debit freight in and other charges to the appropriate expense accounts; debit or credit variance; credit accounts payable; and place the payment data in an accounts payable suspense file or buffer. On the payment date the computer will debit accounts payable, credit cash, and print the check.

Manual versus Computer-Based Systems

The accounts payable example illustrates the interaction and interdependency of and between the accounts payable and cost accounting systems in either a manual or computer-based mode. It also demonstrates the similarity or parallelism of manual and computer processes or frameworks. The manual system frameworks or processes described and illustrated in this book are standard or industry norms for manufacturing systems. Standard or normal manual systems are used to create computer-based systems for a number of reasons: they work; they are familiar to operating people; they make the conversion from manual to computer-based systems relatively simple; they allow manual and computer-based systems to be run in parallel until the conversion has been thoroughly debugged.

Need for Accuracy   A complete, accurate, error-free, up-to-date database is needed in either the manual or the computer-based mode. A defective database can be accommodated in a manual mode: people learn to work around errors. A defective database will kill a computer-based system: the computer assumes that everything is perfect. Accuracy of transactions, called *input,* is important to both manual and computer-based systems. Surprisingly, computer-based systems do a better job than manual systems of ferreting out and calling attention to transaction errors. Computer-based systems contain programs or processes called *parity checks* that disclose transaction errors in the form of an error listing. Computer-based system parity checks are similar in concept to double-entry bookkeeping systems: errors introduced in double-entry bookkeeping systems result in accounts not balancing, which forces a search for and correction of the error.

When the time comes to convert from your manual system to a computer-based system, it is vital to check, double-check, and then triple-check the database before starting the conversion program. Chances are quite high that the accounting system will be the first system to be converted. Problems in converting an accounting system are the tip of the iceberg compared with the problems encountered in converting the inventory and work in process systems. An ounce or two of accounting system conversion problems are forerunners of a ton or two of inventory and work in process system conversion problems.

The Manufacturing-Company Language

Chapter 2 is devoted entirely to the unique language of manufacturing companies. Other chapters discuss the language unique to a specific function. The language discussions are provided to clarify the terminology peculiar to manufacturing companies. Although you may be familiar with the terminology, you may be unsure of exact meanings and, importantly, what these things mean to, and the effect they can have on, the business.

Flowcharts

Flowcharts are to business systems what wiring diagrams or schematics are to electrical or plumbing systems: they enable the peruser to follow the flow of parts, material, and paperwork through a functional business system. Each flowchart is accompanied by a narrative description noting what forms are used and why; who puts what data in what blocks on the form and why; what action steps consist of and why; where documents, parts, or material come from that enter or start the system; and where they go when the system has completed its process.

To illustrate flowchart symbols and how to use and follow flowcharts, we will follow a typical flowchart, Figure 1-1. The flow is left to right. The leftmost symbol indicates the start of the flowchart process. In the example, the process starts with document A affixed to or inside of a box of parts. Document A and the parts remain together, as depicted by the bracket and single flow line. An action step is performed using both document A and the parts. After the action step is performed, document A is separated from the parts. The parts are forwarded to a staging area and are staged on a shelf. Document A is used to create document B. Document A is filed. Document B is forwarded to the document B destination. Completion of the process is depicted by parts and documents being located somewhere in a staging location or file or being forwarded to another destination.

Forms

Chapters 15 and 16 provide sample formats for all database and working documents discussed in the book. They also discuss the need for, use of, and suggested management policy regarding each form. Use the sample forms to design your own or as a guide to purchasing them from an office supplies store. The data blocks included on each form are fairly standard. But the layout of the data blocks should be tailored to your specific needs. The layout of a form that will be filed in a vertical tub file, for example, will be different from that of one filed in a three-ring binder, which will in turn be different from that of one filed in a Kardex.

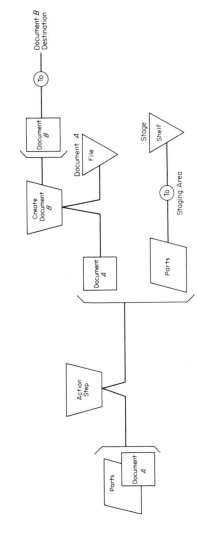

FIGURE 1-1 Typical flowchart

Departmental Operating Manuals

When your firm reaches a size that warrants departmentalization, you will be wise to create an operating manual for each department, and in some cases for subfunctions within a department. There are several equally important reasons, or imperatives, for operating manuals:

They are a training aid for new or temporary employees.

They provide a vehicle that enables departmental employees to understand and comprehend what their department does and how what they do fits the overall departmental system.

They enable employees whose duties require them to interact with several departmental systems to see how each system works.

They reflect your policies, fiats, or edicts of how you expect and demand your employees operate your business.

Your Manufacturing Company is a series of generalized departmental operating manuals. Use it as a guide or baseline to create your own set of operating manuals.

Most employees will work within the system as long as the system allows them to perform their assigned tasks or duties. If something changes that prevents them from accomplishing their mission by adhering to the system, they will ignore the system and work around it. Recognize that conditions will change or something will happen that will require systems to be revised. Be receptive and alert to suggestions for improvements or needed changes. Today's version of a business system is like today's version of your product line. They both have a finite life. They both need periodic revision, revamping, or updating to remain viable and productive.

2

THE MANUFACTURING-
COMPANY LANGUAGE

Except in the very early start-up stage, the manufacturing function is usually larger than all the other functions combined in the size of the work force, floor space, and percentage of the sales dollar it consumes. Manufacturing uses all the database documents described in Chapter 15. Manufacturing creates and uses most of the working documents discussed in Chapter 16.

To the uninitiated, a factory appears to be a mysterious and confusing amorphous mass of parts, material, machines, and people. To replace the mystery with understanding and the confusion with order, the various components of the manufacturing function—material requirements planning, purchasing, work in process, receiving, stockroom, shipping, and quality control—are each discussed in separate chapters. They are all tied together by a language peculiar to manufacturing. This chapter provides much more than just a glossary or definitions of manufacturing terminology. It discusses what the items, entities, and functions defined by manufacturing terminology mean to the business; the effect they can have on the business; and suggestions for controlling them using management policies and decision rules.

BOOKING, SALE

A *booking* is receipt of an order from a customer. A *sale* is shipment of the product and issuance of an invoice to the customer. In the case of a product shipped from stock or finished goods, a booking and a sale, for practical purposes, occur simultaneously. When the product is shipped some days or weeks after receipt of a customer order, bookings will precede sales. The time interval between a booking and the subsequent sale is called *customer lead time* or *delivery time*.

BACKLOG

Backlog is unshipped customer orders. Negative backlog is finished goods. Depending on the marketplace, the type of product, and historical imperatives in your industry, you may elect to operate your business with a planned backlog of unshipped orders or to operate it from a finished goods position, where shipment is made immediately upon receipt of a customer order. If the business operates from a planned backlog position, management and marketing should establish a backlog policy: backlog should be planned at not less than X weeks and not more than Y weeks. If the business is operated from a finished goods position, management and marketing should establish a finished goods policy: finished goods should be planned within X units minimum and Y units maximum.

RESERVATIONS

A business with a product line that has numerous options tends to operate from a backlog position because each customer order could be for a different configuration, and that configuration will not be known until the order is booked. If finished goods are created, they will probably need to be altered at additional expense to match a customer order.

However, even though finished goods are undesirable, the time will inevitably come when existing backlog does not fill the monthly build-ship schedule. The *build-ship schedule* is a list of the quantity of each specific model number scheduled to be built and shipped in a given month. The option of halting production until orders arrive is unacceptable. Therefore, when backlog is not sufficient to fill the month's build-ship schedule, marketing should reserve product configurations that match orders they anticipate booking in time to ship during the current build-ship month. A reservation system is also useful when the backlog of unshipped orders is high. By reserving a portion of the build-ship schedule, marketing will have some units available for faster than normal delivery. Quick delivery is often the deciding factor in whether you or a competitor get the order.

LEAD TIME LIST

The *lead time list* notes the lead time for major categories of purchased items. It should be issued periodically by purchasing as conditions in the marketplace change. It is a tool for inventory analysis enabling the business to accommodate varying vendor lead times in the purchased parts and material planning and ordering process.

INVENTORY

There are several types or classifications of *inventory*. Each one is planned, managed, and accounted for differently. The traditional measure of inventory management is the *inventory turn ratio*. The turn ratio is the yearly cost of inventory divided by the average monthly inventory value. For example, if $100 is expended for a given inventory classification each year and the average monthly value of that classification is $25, the turn ratio is $4 : {}^{100}\!/_{25} = 4$. Generally, the higher the turn ratio, the better inventory is being managed.

Stockroom Inventory

Stockroom inventory is an accounting classification and a physical location. The stockroom may or may not have walls, but it should be a distinct area of floor space or specified shelving units. The stockroom may also have an annex or two to accommodate outsized parts or material. Parts, material, and assemblies are transacted into the stockroom via receipts from vendors or stock transfers from completed work orders or other inventory classifications. They are transacted out of the stockroom via manufactured-part and assembly work orders and stock requisitions.

The level of stockroom inventory is controlled through ordering rules imposed on the material requirements planning function. Good control of high-dollar-value part numbers, called A-value part numbers, can turn stockroom inventory up to 6 times per year.

Work in Process Inventory

Work in process inventory, called WIP, is an accounting classification. WIP includes parts, material, and assemblies that have been transacted into an open work order or subcontract. WIP is physically located in a staging area, in a factory department, or at a subcontractor. Parts, material, and assemblies are transacted from WIP to other inventory classifications via a stock transfer.

As discussed in Chapter 9, "Work in Process," subassembly work orders are typically issued 3 months ahead of the month in which they are scheduled to be assembled in the final product and shipped. This allows

1 month to pick and kit the work order in the stockroom, 1 month to expedite and fill shortages, and 1 month to physically assemble the subassembly. This type of lead time is called *lead time setback*. The phrase "lead time setback of ship minus three" means that the lead time for issuing the work order is 3 months ahead of the month in which the final product is scheduled to be shipped.

The level of WIP is controlled by the length of time open work orders are allowed to languish in WIP. Theoretically, with a lead time setback policy of ship minus three for subassembly parts, no work order will be more than 3 months old, which equates to 4 turns. In practice, work orders tend to be worked on when they appear on a short sheet. If they don't bubble up on a short sheet, they literally gather dust as they grow older and older. A policy of completing open work orders within 1 month of their due date or crediting them back to the stockroom is recommended.

Finished Goods Inventory

Finished goods is an accounting classification. Finished goods are physically located in a designated area of floor space or shelving units. Transactions into finished goods are usually via a stock transfer from a completed work order. A customer invoice or debit memo is the usual vehicle to transact finished goods to cost of sales or consignment inventory.

The level of finished goods and the finished goods turn ratio are controlled by the minimum-maximum policy imposed on the material requirements planning function.

Consignment Inventory

Consignment inventory is an accounting classification used in the situation when product is consigned to a customer or sales representative. The transaction to consignment inventory is usually a debit memo. The transaction from consignment inventory is either a customer invoice or a credit memo.

Spare Parts Inventory

Spare parts inventory is an accounting classification. Spare parts are stocked to cover scrap generated in the production process and for postsale product support. They are stored in a designated area of floor space or shelving units. Transactions into spare parts inventory are usually receipts from vendors or transfers from completed work orders. A customer invoice or stock requisition transacts spare parts inventory to cost of sales or an open work order.

In a start-up situation using a job-lot material requirements planning system, a separate spare parts accounting classification and physical location makes sense. In an ongoing situation using a forecast-demand material requirements planning system, a separate spare parts accounting classification or physical location is not necessary. The periodic ordering cycle including field service requirements normally accommodates all spare parts usage.

Repair-Exchange Inventory

Repair-exchange inventory includes modules or subassemblies such as motors, pumps, valves, or circuit cards that have ceased to function in the field and have been rebuilt in the factory. For example, a burned-out motor can be rebuilt to perform like a new motor by rewinding the rotor and stator and installing new bearings. Repair-exchange is covered in depth in Chapter 5, "Post-Sale Support and Product Liability."

Obsolete Inventory

Obsolete inventory is an expense against profit when it is physically scrapped or disposed of. Obsolete inventory is generated when an engineering change order makes a part number obsolete and is the residual value of unique parts left over when a product is phased out of production.

When a decision has been made to phase out a product, compiling a list of parts in inventory that are unique to that product and analyzing it is recommended. The analysis should determine that quantity of product that should be produced to reduce the residual value of leftover unique parts to a reasonable minimum, and the phaseout program should be planned accordingly. Most computer-based inventory systems contain a unique parts explosion capability to plan product phaseout programs.

When part numbers become obsolete through an engineering change order or product phaseout program, the prudent business practice is to write them off and physically dispose of them.

Book Inventory

Book inventory is the value of inventory reflected on the balance sheet at the close of an accounting period. It is calculated by adding all dollars transacted into inventory during an accounting period to the book inventory as of the prior accounting period and deducting all dollar transactions out of inventory during the accounting period. It is alternatively calculated by extending the on-hand balance of inventory records by standard cost.

Physical Inventory

The term *physical inventory* has two different usages or meanings. It is the actual quantity physically on hand, and it is also the task of periodically counting what is physically on hand. Businesses periodically verify the physical inventory by taking (counting) a physical inventory. The physical inventory is normally taken at the end of the fiscal year.

Inventory Reserve

Over time, total physical inventory tends to shrink and, despite efforts to control engineering changes and product phaseout programs, to generate an obsolete component. Inventory shrinkage and obsolescence is a fact of manufacturing life and is coped with by establishing a reserve for shrinkage and obsolescence. Shrinkage and obsolescence is not a problem in a start-up situation using a job-lot material requirements planning system, and a reserve is really not needed or recommended in this situation. At some point on the growth curve a reserve for shrinkage and obsolescence makes sense. Most certified public accounting firms will insist on one when the time comes for certified financial statements. One way to get at how large the reserve should be is with a cycle counting program.

Inventory Cycle Counting

As previously discussed, most manufacturing companies take a physical inventory at the close of their fiscal year for two reasons: first, to adjust on-hand balances in inventory records to what is physically in the stockroom, work in process, and finished goods; second, to correctly value inventory. More times than not, the year-end adjustment to on-hand balances and inventory value tends to be relatively large. An inventory cycle counting program enables the company to make smaller adjustments periodically as the year unfolds; this will avoid the unpleasant surprise of a large year-end adjustment that, in many cases, wreaks havoc with the year's profit, not to mention disclosing an unbalanced inventory.

Inventory cycle counting programs are normally restricted to stockroom inventory and are quite simple to implement. First, ensure that all stockroom inventory transactions are posted at the close of the work week. Second, using a random-numbers table, make a list of part numbers to be cycle counted. Third, count the physical quantity for each part number on the list. Fourth, compare the physical count with the inventory record on-hand balance. If the on-hand balance and the physical count are relatively close, adjust the on-hand balance to the physical count. If there is a large discrepancy, verify the physical count before making the adjustment. The quantity of part numbers to be counted should be limited to the number that can be processed prior to resuming work the following week. Part-time college students are good cycle counters.

The 80-20 rule, discussed in the A, B, C value category paragraph, suggests that controlling the high-value A parts will control the bulk of the total inventory value. Cycle counting A-value parts once every month and adjusting the book inventory value to the value of the physical count will keep the book and physical inventory values relatively close. The probability is quite high that the adjustments will tend to reduce the book inventory value. The dollar value of these cycle-count adjustments can be the basis for determining the amount of inventory reserve that will be needed to cover shrinkage. The amount needed to cover obsolescence is a judgment call. A cycle-counting rule of thumb is to count all A-value parts once a month, all B-value parts two or three times a year, and C-value parts once a year.

INVENTORY FUNCTION

The inventory function includes the planning necessary to make the required quantity of piece parts and assemblies available on the date they are needed.

PRODUCTION FUNCTION

The production function takes requirements for manufactured parts and assemblies from the inventory function, causes parts to be manufactured or assembled, and transacts them as they move through the manufacturing process. The production function includes planning to assure sufficient work force, space, and necessary tools are available, together with the scheduling and control functions to assure timely completion of manufactured-part and assembly work orders.

STAGING

Staging is the term describing placement of parts and material or work orders in a staging or holding area pending release to the next function or operation. A *staging area* is a designated area of floor space or shelving units. To stage something means to put it in a staging area.

INVENTORY ANALYSIS

Inventory analysis is the part of the overall forecast-demand material requirements planning process that determines requirements for each part number. Tools used in inventory analysis include on-hand assemblies and parts, on-order assemblies and parts, master schedule, short sheets, lead time setback, lead time list, A, B, C ordering rules, special ordering rules, and service parts requirements.

UNIT OF MEASURE

Unit of measure is the dimension used to describe raw material items such as sheet stock, bar or rod stock, wire, tubing, and finishing materials.

When you start your company, establish a unit of measure policy and follow it; e.g., for sheet stock, determine whether you will specify it with a length and width dimension or in square inches or square feet. For bar stock or rod stock, decide whether you will use inches, feet, or pounds.

UNIQUE OR COMMON PARTS

A part is unique as long as it is used on only one assembly. A unique part becomes a common part the instant it becomes used on a second assembly. Common parts are parts that are used on two or more different assemblies.

M-A-P

The part number register, used-on register, and bill of material provide for coding each part number M for manufactured, A for assembly, or P for purchased. The inventory function needs the M-A-P coding to determine how to order the part.

To the inventory, production, receiving, stockroom, and other manufacturing functions of larger ongoing companies, a part number is a part number is a part number. These people do not have much opportunity to associate "part number X, base, filter separator" with the actual physical part. In fact, they would not recognize a filter separator base if one bit them on the ankle. Their interest in part number X is whether it is purchased, manufactured, or assembled; whether it is unique to a single product or is common to a number of products; what its value classification is so that they know how many to order and how to schedule receipts. The paperwork required to order purchased parts is different from that for manufactured parts is different from that for assemblies.

PLANNING PERIOD

A *planning period* is a period of time, usually a calendar month, in which discrete manufacturing functions are planned and executed, e.g., pulling, staging, filling shorts, and assembling assembly work orders.

ECONOMIC ORDER QUANTITY

The *economic order quantity,* or *EOQ,* is a key factor in inventory control and cost of sales. It is applied in one form or another in each ordering decision. Briefly, EOQ treats the following two factors:

- Procuring or fabricating larger quantities of piece parts tends to lower piece part cost.

- The more you order, the longer they last and the more it will cost to carry them in inventory.

The EOQ decision process balances piece part cost against cost to carry; it is graphically illustrated in Figure 2-1.

The form of EOQ application varies from judgment calls based on experience to complex computerized analyses. There are a myriad of EOQ formulas and applications available in publications treating inventory theory.

EOQ does not make sense for a start-up business. It does make sense for an ongoing business that has reached a size that warrants a separate inventory function department. A, B, C ordering rules, to be discussed next, are a much better, prudent, real-world approach to establishing quantities for start-up and small ongoing businesses.

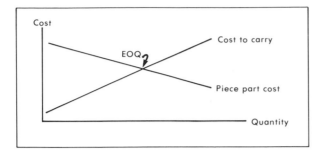

FIGURE 2-1   Economic order quantity

A, B, C VALUE CATEGORIES

The 80-20 rule applies nearly universally to any inventory. Briefly, the 80-20 rule states that 80 percent of the annual dollar expenditure for inventory is represented in 20 percent of the part numbers in the part number population. If you have 1000 part numbers and cost of sales is $1,000,000, $800,000 is represented in 200 part numbers. It follows that controlling the 200 high-value parts will control the bulk of cost of sales.

If you rank-order your inventory population with the part number representing the highest yearly dollar expenditure on top and the part number representing the lowest annual dollar expenditure on the bottom, you can arbitrarily divide that rank-order list into three sections. The high-dollar-volume portion of inventory on the top of the list is labeled A value; the extremely low-dollar-value parts on the bottom of the list are labeled C value; and the population of part numbers between the A cutoff and the C cutoff are labeled B value.

When you are a small ongoing business, it may not be practical or even feasible to prepare a yearly dollar-value rank-order list of inventory. Someone in the organization can apply judgment calls to the part number population and arbitrarily assign an A, B, C value to each part number. Chances are that if the arbitrary classification could be compared with an actual rank-order listing, they would be extremely close. They will certainly be close enough for the real world. Make a judgment call on how many part numbers can be analyzed and cycle-counted each month to determine the quantity of A-value part numbers your system can handle. Make another judgment call on what annual dollar usage value will constitute a C-value classification. The part numbers between the A and C cutoffs are B value. A cycle-counting rule of thumb is to count all A-value parts once a month, B-value parts two or three times a year, and C-value parts once a year.

ORDERING RULES

Ordering rules are management policies that impose limits within which various functions and levels in the organization order parts, material, supplies, and sundries. Some suggested ordering rules follow.

A Value

Cover vendor lead time plus 3 months' usage. Schedule receipts monthly.

B Value

Order and schedule receipt of 3 months' usage in one shipment.

C Value

Order and schedule receipt of 6 months' usage in one shipment.

A, B, C Approval Level

Purchases can be approved by the inventory analyst up to $X;$ production manager approval is needed for purchases between X and Y total value: the president must approve purchases above Y total value.

Nonproduction Items Approval Level

Purchases can be approved by the department head up to X total value; the president must approve purchases above X total value.

SPECIAL ORDERING RULES

Some items may require special ordering rules. Some vendors, for instance, will ship only in quantities of 100 and will refuse to accept an order of, say, 78 or 104, and will send it back. In these rare cases special ordering rules should be written down on paper and provided to the inventory analyst.

QUEUE TIME

Queue time is time consumed by the system in such functions as generating paperwork, approvals, clerical backlog, or moving paperwork from one department to another. As shown in Figure 2-2, the purchasing process queue time can exceed the vendor lead time.

LEAD TIME SETBACK

Lead time setback is the part of the inventory analysis process that schedules inventory events to coincide with your production flow. A typical production flow is shown in Figure 2-3.

Lead time setback for receipt of final assembly parts is the number of planning periods required to accommodate pulling and staging final assembly kits, filling shortages, building the final assembly, and testing the product. Receipt of subassembly parts must be scheduled ahead of receipt of final assembly parts because subassemblies must be pulled, staged, shortages filled, and the subassembly completed to coincide with receipt of final assembly parts.

SHORTS

Inventory and production planning is not an exact science. Theoretically, if everything goes according to plan, each part will be received on the day requested, none will be rejected, sufficient work force will be trained and available for assembly, no scrap will be generated, the product will work, service will not exceed the forecast demand, no parts or assemblies will be lost, and so on. However, if something can go wrong it will ... therefore, there will be shortages.

Rarely is an assembly kit pulled complete. Some shortages, either partial or zero fills, are par for the course and must be coped with. The typical method of coping with shortages is to generate a *short sheet,* Figure 16-16, which is a list of part numbers that are short and the work orders that need them. The short sheet is used to expedite receipt of short parts.

GROSS REQUIREMENT

The *gross requirement* for a part number in a given planning period is the total quantity of that part number that is to ship, assembled in the finished product, during the planning period.

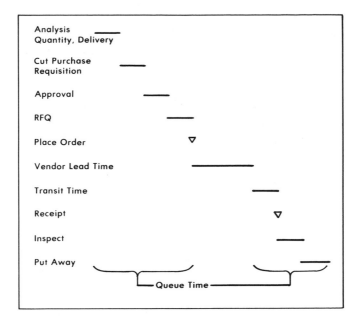

FIGURE 2-2   Queue time

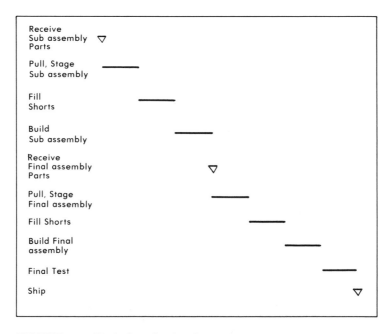

FIGURE 2-3   Typical production flow

GROSS GROSS REQUIREMENT

The *gross gross requirement* for a part number is the gross requirement plus shortages.

NET REQUIREMENT

The *net requirement* for a part number in a given planning period is the gross gross requirement minus the balance on hand, minus parts in completed subassemblies, minus parts in open work orders. If the net available exceeds the gross requirement for planning period 1, the balance on hand is applied to the gross requirement of following planning periods.

NET NET REQUIREMENT

The *net net requirement* for a part number is the net requirement adjusted for lead time setback. Net net requirements are the quantity of parts required to be available per planning period.

PART TWO
THE PRODUCT LINE, THE MARKETPLACE

To your customers—those that have purchased your product and those that are contemplating purchasing your product—your company is the product line, the people that sell and service it, and your reputation for post-sale product and customer support. Customers have little or no interest in your facility or the people that toil within its six walls designing and manufacturing the product line. Their purchasing decision is made on the basis of the merits of your product versus those of competitive products, the behavior of your sales representatives, and the perception of how well they and the product will be supported after they have made their purchase.

The three chapters in Part 2—"The Product Line," "Marketing," and "Post-Sale Product Support and Product Liability"—cover the functions that determine your success, or lack thereof, in your marketplace.

CHAPTER 3: THE PRODUCT LINE

This chapter covers the product selection process, the product design process, new product introduction, and how to cope with specials.

CHAPTER 4: MARKETING

This chapter discusses the conduit between the marketplace and your company, including securing and qualifying sales leads and converting them to orders; finding, qualifying, and managing sales representatives;

quotations and sales orders; and coping with international or overseas markets.

CHAPTER 5: POST-SALE PRODUCT SUPPORT AND PRODUCT LIABILITY

This chapter covers product liability considerations: product liability insurance, recall-retrofit programs, and limited warranty. It also discusses post-sale product and customer support: customer training, product installation, and warranty and post-warranty service; how to locate, train, and manage service representatives; and a repair-exchange program and control of serial-numbered items.

3
THE PRODUCT LINE

A successful product line fits the marketplace and is profitable. A good marketplace fit causes customers to buy your products in preference to competitive products. Profit generates cash, which makes growth and expansion possible.

This chapter concentrates on the product selection process, which is a sequential series of go or no-go decision points that assist in the ultimate product line decision of which products to continue in the line, which products to phase out of the line, and, importantly, which products to add to the line. All products have a finite life cycle that can be pictured as a graph with unit and dollar volume on the vertical axis and time in years on the horizontal axis. The typical life-cycle curve starts with the first sale. Initial growth is relatively slow until the new product gains market acceptance. Once the product gains acceptance, the growth curve accelerates and ultimately reaches its apogee. The curve may remain on a high plateau for some period of time or may immediately commence its descent into oblivion and obsolescence. It is important to acknowledge the fact that all products *do* have a finite life and to recognize when it is time to phase out the old in favor of the new. The name of the game in the product selection process is to plan the phaseout of old products, the continuation of products that are alive and healthy, and the introduction of new products in a fashion that keeps the composite growth curve of the entire product line headed in a positive direction. The composite product line growth curve is the company's growth curve.

The marketplace determines the shape of the composite product line or company growth curve. Marketplace input is transmitted to the prod-

Booking-Sales Forecast										Date	FEB	
Product/Model	Jan	Feb	Mar	Apr	May	Jun	Jul	Aug	Sep	Oct	Nov	Dec
A	—	10	12	12	8	8	6	4	2	—	—	—
B	28	20	20	22	24	26	26	26	26	28	28	28
C	10	—	2	4	6	8	10	10	10	10	10	10

FIGURE 3-1   Booking-sales forecast

uct selection process via the periodic booking-sales forecast, Figure 3-1, created by marketing.

In the Figure 3-1 example, orders for product *A* are projected to peak in March and April. They turn downward starting in May to product *A's* demise in September. Product *B* is alive, healthy, and still in its ascendancy mode. The first orders for new product *C* are anticipated in March. The company response to this marketplace input is to phase out product *A*, adjust production schedules for product *B* to satisfy order input, and assure that product *C* is available to satisfy the March orders. Fortunately, in the case of product *A*, manufacturing management has 8 months' lead time to plan its phaseout program so that a minimum level of obsolete product *A* inventory is written off against profit. The remainder of this chapter concentrates on the new product selection process, the product design process, new product introduction, and a way to handle specials to satisfy the inevitable order that specifies, just like the catalog, except. . .

THE NEW PRODUCT SELECTION PROCESS

Prior to or immediately subsequent to becoming a start-up company, you probably conducted a very comprehensive new product project planning process that culminated in the business plan that secured financing and got you underway. To assure the viability of future new products, a similar, though much less comprehensive, exercise is recommended.

Although new product ideas can emanate from a variety of sources, they normally bubble up in engineering or marketing. Assuming that a new product idea will be a major or at least a significant addition to the product line, the new product project planning process makes sense. It provides a vehicle to discipline the organization to thoroughly think through all aspects of the project: is it technically feasible, can it be manufactured at the estimated cost, and will it sell at the recommended price in the projected quantity?

A new product project should be initiated for each new product idea deemed worthy of consideration as a potential addition to the product line. Project planning includes product definition, product cost, capital cost, pricing, and financial evaluation.

Product Definition

The first step in product definition is to convert the new product idea into a customer specification. The customer specification should take the form of a rough draft of a product brochure or catalog, including sketches and recommended pricing based on the marketplace, not on manufacturing costs. It is recommended that the customer specification be field-tested with seasoned sales representatives and knowledgeable customers or users to provide some real-world reaction to the concept. Assuming that the field reaction is favorable, the product configuration and pricing parameters of the new product equation are tentatively established.

The second step is an engineering specification that will govern the design to meet the customer specification requirements. Typically, this is the juncture at which tradeoffs between customer specifications and technical specifications occur. For example, to meet the customer specification of $\pm 1\%$ will require an extra 6 months' development time and will increase product cost by X percent. If $\pm 2\%$ is satisfactory, the desired time schedule and product cost can be met. The engineering specification also defines product serviceability. Serviceability, or how the product will be serviced in the field, is a key parameter in the customer specification and the engineering specification. Serviceability parameters must be included in the product design and documentation. They include:

- To what extent and precisely what repairs can be performed by the customer? What level of service will require a trained professional?

- Will field repair be limited to module replacement, or will troubleshooting to the component level be planned?

- What level of required preventive maintenance can be performed by the customer and what level requires a trained professional?

- Will the product be shipped completely assembled and ready for operation, or will it be shipped partially assembled? Can the customer assemble it, or will assembly and checkout on site require a trained professional?

- Will a spare parts kit be included in the shipping assembly?

- What level of spare parts will be stocked at the customer's facility, at your service representative, and in the factory spare parts inventory?

In a start-up situation the serviceability considerations are easily decided . . . you make all the decisions. In a larger ongoing company with separate marketing, engineering, and service functions, you will be wise to convene your entire new product team and assure a meeting of the minds on serviceability before you launch the new product project. Product design revisions to accommodate different serviceability requirements after the product design is completed can be expensive.

Product Cost and Capital Cost

Product cost and capital cost are key parameters in the financial evaluation of profitability and the return on investment in new product development projects. The product cost and capital cost estimating tools include the xmas tree, bills of material, and a meeting-of-the-minds dialog between engineering and manufacturing. The first tool is the xmas tree, Figure 3-2.

The xmas tree pictures how the product will be structured. It should include a box for each anticipated bill of material for all planned options and for subassemblies at each level of assembly. Make sure that marketing, service, engineering, and manufacturing all agree with the product structure from the outset of the project. The next step is bills of material, Figure 3-3.

A tentative bill of material should be prepared for each assembly that will be stocked as a separate entity. Note the description and M-A-P code for each part, assembly, or material item anticipated to be included in the design of the assembly covered by the bill of material. Recognize that the tentative bill of material is indeed tentative, but make it as comprehensive and accurate as possible.

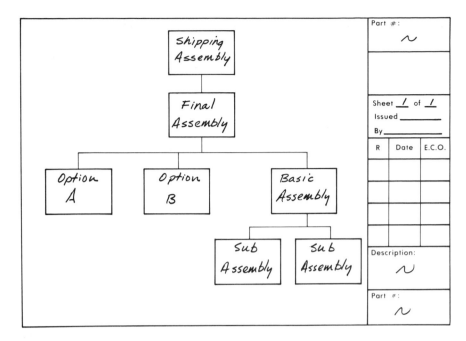

FIGURE 3-2   Xmas tree

		Part #	Description	M A P	Qty		Part #:
1							
2							
3							Bill of Material
4							Sheet ___ of ___ Issued _____
5							By _____
6							Rev. Date E.C.O.
7							
8							
9							
10							
11							Description:
12							
13							
14							Part #:
15							

FIGURE 3-3   Bill of material

The next step is the meeting-of-the-minds dialog between engineering and manufacturing. The dialog consists of patiently and thoroughly discussing each line item on each page of each bill of material. The objective is to arrive at a meeting of the minds between engineering and manufacturing on what is needed to manufacture or procure each line item: engineering drawing, standard tooling, special tooling including tool design and fabrication, jigs, test fixtures, test equipment, engineering specification, process specification, test procedure, vendor part number, fabrication hours, assembly hours, test hours, and so on.

When the tentative bills of material reflect the combined wisdom of engineering and manufacturing, engineering can use the data to prepare the engineering project authority, Figure 3-4, which is a layout of the engineering resources required to bring the new product on stream.

Manufacturing can use the data to compile a product cost estimate of purchased parts and material, manufactured parts, and assembly costs for the basic product and all options. Cost data are also available for spare parts and repair-exchange items.

Engineering Project Authority _____   Description _____

		1	2	3	4	5	6	7	8	9	10	11	12	Total
Mechanical Engineer	Hours													
	$													
Electrical Engineer	Hours													
	$													
Drafting	Hours													
	$													
Technician	Hours													
	$													
Other	Hours													
	$													
Material	$													
Other Expense	$													
Total	Hours													
	$													
Key Events														

1. _____   3. _____   Customer Spec. _____

Engineering Spec. _____ | | Approved | Date |

2. _____   4. _____   Financial Evaluation _____   R&D ___ ___   Mktg ___ ___   Mfg ___ ___

FIGURE 3-4   Engineering project authority

Pricing

This discussion of pricing will attempt to make the case for pricing your product at what it is worth to the customer rather than applying some arbitrary mark-up to cost. Your pricing policy should include a preordained minimum gross margin ratio between cost and selling price and a preordained return on investment ratio for all new product programs.

Competitive Comparison Matrix A *competitive comparison matrix* is a tool that is helpful in the pricing process. Mechanically, a competitive comparison matrix is a piece of paper with significant product features or specifications, including a line for prices, listed one under the other in a column on the left margin. There is a column for your new product and a column for each product it will compete with. The matrix provides an overview of how your product compares with competitive products on price and major features or specifications. Although it is highly desirable to have all specifications and features of your new product significantly better than competitive products, development and product cost tradeoffs may not give you the luxury of having the ideal product. Your product should have more pluses than minuses compared with the competition. A "me too" product rarely captures a significant market share. A competitive comparison matrix is admittedly a subjective tool to compare your product's attributes and pricing with those of competitive products. Despite the subjective nature of a competitive comparison matrix, generating it is a good discipline for marketing, as it requires them to think through all facets of the customer specification. It also provides you with a good feel for where your price level should be relative to competitive products.

Price-Feature Totem Pole Another tool that is helpful in the pricing process is a *price-feature totem pole*. A price-feature totem pole is constructed by simply drawing a vertical line on a piece of paper. Label the top of the line "highest price" and the bottom of the line "lowest price." If you were totem-poling automobiles, Cadillac and Lincoln would be toward the top of the line, Mercury and Oldsmobile would be sort of in the middle, and Chevrolet and Ford would be toward the bottom of the line. Slot your new product and competitive products on the price-feature totem pole to get another qualitative measure of where your product price and features should rank with competitive products.

Ancillary Item Pricing   It is recommended that ancillary items, such as consumables, spare parts, and repair-exchange items, also be priced on the basis of worth to the customer rather than at an arbitrary mark-up on cost.

Consumables   Pricing of consumables used with your product is highly dependent on their availability to the customer. If your company is the only one that provides consumables, price them as high as you can without scaring off the customer. If consumables are very easily available to the customer, your price may need to be lower than that of your competition if it requires more effort for the customer to buy from you than from a more readily available local source. In this case, you may be wise not to fuss with consumables, but to devote your energies to selling the product proper.

Spare Parts   Someone once calculated that a $5000 automobile purchased as spare parts would cost more than $25,000. Demand for spare parts is extremely inelastic. A customer needing a spare part will, within reason, pay any price for it. Customers are acclimated to paying high prices for spare parts.

By definition, unique parts fabricated to your specifications or drawings are available only from your company. It is recommended that you price unique spare parts somewhat higher than what you would consider exorbitant.

You should note the manufacturer and manufacturer part number for spare parts that are standard catalog items in your maintenance manual to encourage customers and service representatives to buy them direct and not from you. Customers do balk at paying a premium for something that is readily available to them, and so profit from standard catalog spare parts will be slim or nonexistent.

Repair-Exchange Items   As discussed in Chapter 5, "Post-Sale Support and Product Liability," repair-exchange items generally command a price in the vicinity of 60 percent of the price of a new item. Some customers have an aversion to buying a used anything. You will need a price for new items that are also available as repair-exchange items. Because these items tend to be unique, their price should be at the unique part level.

Financial Evaluation

The financial evaluation form, Figure 3-5, is a mini-business plan for each new product project.

Net sales are derived from a unit sales forecast and pricing recommended by marketing. Cost of sales is compiled by manufacturing from data on the tentative bills of material. Expenses are normally calculated

Financial Evaluation					
EPA _____ Description _____					
By _____ Date_____					
List Price $ _____	Year 1	Year 2	Year 3	__ Years	Total
1. Unit Sales					
2. Net Price $ _____					
3. Net Sales (1x2)					
4. Direct Labor $					
5. Burden (@ %) $					
6. Material $					
7. Cost of Sales (4+5+6)					
8. Gross Profit (3-7)					
9. Sales Expense					
10. G&A Expense					
11. Other Expense					
12. Total Expense (9+10+11)					
13. NBT (8-12)					
14. NBT % (13/3)					
Investment					
15. R&D $					
16. Tooling $					
17. Inventory (7/Turns) $					
18. Receivables (@ % Sales) $					
19. Total Investment (15+16+17+18)					
20. R.O.I. (13/19)					
Approvals:					
Marketing Engineering Manufacturing ———————					
By_____ Date____ By_____Date____ By_____Date___ By_____ Date___					

FIGURE 3-5   Financial evaluation

using the current expense-to-sales ratios. R&D and tooling costs are provided by engineering from the engineering project authority and data on the tentative bills of material. Inventory is cost of sales, line 7, divided by the current inventory turns ratio. Receivables are net sales extended by the current ratio of receivables to sales.

If the financial evaluation meets or exceeds your preordained ratios, you can commission the development of a viable product. If, on the other hand, your preordained ratios are not met, you can scrap the project or send marketing, engineering, and manufacturing back to the drawing board.

PRODUCT DESIGN

The specific product design process is, of course, dependent on the product being developed. The output of the design process is a set of database documents that define the product so that it can be manufactured. To assure that final documentation does reflect a manufacturable product, it is recommended that a pilot production lot be manufactured, assembled, and tested by engineering technicians. The objective of the pilot production lot is to debug or correct errors in the documentation before it is turned over to manufacturing.

NEW PRODUCT INTRODUCTION

When you are a start-up company, the response time between committing a new product program and getting it on stream is extremely fast. All hands are intimately involved and aware of every bit of progress and every problem or obstacle encountered. When problems are encountered, all hands rally round to resolve them. Inevitably, as the company grows and additional people come on board, the response time tends to slow down and become interminable.

The decay in new product response time can be avoided by re-creating the start-up company environment with a new product team. The purpose of the new product team is to eliminate, as much as possible, time consumed by the system in completing the design, documentation, engineering or prototype model construction, testing, debugging, and final release of a salable and manufacturable new product. Each department or function that will contribute to the design, development, manufacture, sale, installation, and service should provide a member. The members should have the clout to commit their time and their department to the project and not have commitments subsequently altered. Members must balance project demands with demands of the bread-and-butter product line. Members perform their normal company function unless they can do something quicker and as well as the normal resource. For example, should the service function create the maintenance manual rather than engineering?

Frequent get-togethers and open, candid sharing of data, progress, and problems is the name of the game for a new product team. Basic paper tools include the project schedule, xmas tree, and bills of material. As the design process proceeds and tentative parts become firm, get them on order as soon as possible after engineering says it is okay. Set aside some floor space and shelving to accumulate parts and material separate from the big stockroom. Do not conform to normal systems and procedures unless they are the quickest way. As soon as something firms up, do it. Do not wait for a complete release. Accomplish as much as possible as soon as possible. If some function has a problem you can help with, volunteer. In other words, behave like you are a start-up company.

SPECIALS

There is good news and bad news regarding specials. The good news is that they can be an excellent test for proving out a new product extension or improvement. The bad news is that they are disruptive. They divert precious engineering resources from planned new product development; they interfere with normal factory operations, tend to pose continuing field service problems, and are rarely, if ever, profitable. Inevitably there will be specials, and they must be coped with. The following recommendations for handling specials assume that they are meant to be profitable.

Assure a meeting of the minds between marketing, the customer, engineering, and manufacturing. Use the engineering project authority form, Figure 3-4, to estimate the engineering and manufacturing cost and the delivery schedule for pricing the special to the customer. Use the sales order number as the special job number to collect engineering and manufacturing costs associated with the special; they should be compared with the estimate to sharpen your estimating skills for costing future specials.

Provide the absolute minimum of documentation that the factory can live with:

- A special job bill of material calling out standard product and special job documentation. The special job bill of material serves as the special job part number register.

- Marked-up existing documentation with the "Special Job" stamp, Figure 16-36, affixed.

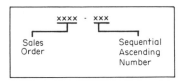

FIGURE 3-6   Special-job part number

- Freehand sketches with the job number followed by sequentially ascending numbers, as in Figure 3-6.

Do not clutter up the ongoing product documentation and part-number systems with specials. Preserve all special job documentation in a special job file in engineering to serve as a baseline for a new product project in the event the special becomes a standard product.

4
MARKETING

Marketing is the interface or conduit between the marketplace and your company. As such, marketing performs the dual role of serving as your company's advocate to the marketplace and serving as the advocate of the marketplace to your company. As the company advocate, marketing promotes your product line via advertising, sales promotion, and sales calls to produce orders. It also plays a key role in post-sale support of the customer and the product to ensure customer satisfaction, which aids the receivable collection process, secures follow-on orders, and, importantly, provides positive references to other potential customers.

As the marketplace advocate to your company, marketing provides feedback on the product line: which products to phase out, which to continue and at what rate, and what the marketplace is looking for in the way of new products. Marketing also fills the ancillary role of gathering intelligence on your competitors' activity.

In a start-up situation, marketing will be one of the many hats you will wear unless one of your partners is a marketing professional. If a professional marketer is not part of your start-up cadre, it is strongly recommended that you add one as soon as you can possibly afford it. With or without a marketing professional, the odds are very high that you will personally close or book the first order. The odds are even higher that you will devote more of your time to marketing than to any other single business function in the early months. Customers and sales representatives are the key people in the marketing process. Because customers and sales representatives are not employees and are not physically at your elbow, they both require an inordinate amount of follow-up.

When you reach the ongoing stage and have a marketing professional on board, you should continue to budget a reasonable amount of your time for the marketing function and discipline yourself to spend it. The marketplace is a key factor in the survival and growth of the enterprise. Frequent and direct contact with the marketplace is a requisite for intelligent decision making on what new products to develop and how many existing products to manufacture. The main thrust of the marketing function is outward to the marketplace. Your marketing policy and practice should emphasize and reinforce this outward thrust. On the other hand, marketing input to the internal functions of new product development, forecasting future bookings and sales, and pricing is also necessary.

Because it is more of an art than a science, there have probably been more words written about marketing than about any other business function. Most of these words take the form of books or trade journal articles that discuss such marketing art forms as advertising, image building, sales promotion, customer psychology, and salesmanship. Esoteric art form that it is, marketing is also a business function. As a business function it requires administration and needs managing. This chapter addresses the mundane marketing administration, management, and follow-up systems for booking orders, managing sales representatives, quotations and sales orders, and some suggestions on how to cope with international or overseas markets.

BOOKING ORDERS

Marketing programs produce sales leads. Sales leads produce booked orders. Traditional marketing programs—such as advertising, sales promotion, direct mail, trade shows, conventions, and seminars—are well treated in publications covering the marketing art form. This discussion of marketing programs will provide some suggestions on how to reach your market or customers at minimum cost and how to convert sales leads to booked orders.

Advertising agencies are experts in creating attractive product brochures and space advertising. They are also relatively expensive. Some typesetters or small printing companies are capable of creating an acceptable layout for brochures or paid advertising and are considerably less expensive.

Even though you cannot afford an advertising agency, it does not cost anything to have an exploratory discussion with one or several of them. Before you set up an exploratory discussion, make sure that the advertising agency has a publication called *Business Publication Rates and Data.*

Business Publication Rates and Data, for practical purposes, has a listing for every professional and trade journal published in the world. The listings provide a vast amount of data on each journal:

- Publisher's name, address, and phone number

- The publisher's editorial statement, which includes a brief summary of the management level or professional discipline of subcribers, subject categories of articles, regular features, special features, etc.

- Data on the cost of various sizes of advertising

- Circulation broken down geographically and by professional discipline of subscribers

It is suggested that you thoroughly research *Business Publication Rates and Data* and make a list of all journals that, according to the publisher's editorial statement, are aimed at your potential customers. Most journals are anxious to provide you with a media kit and a no-charge subscription. A media kit is essentially a catalog of what the journal offers advertisers. In addition to running paid advertising, most journals have direct mail programs that can be tailored to your specific needs.

Many journals include a new product section and provide instructions in the media kit on how to write up a press release covering your new product for insertion in their new product section. There is usually no charge for including you in the new product section. If your new product is deemed of sufficient interest, they may give it cover-story treatment. Some journals are published by or for trade or professional associations that sponsor trade shows or conventions. Perusal of the various journals read by your potential customers can provide you with a good database on competitors and current trends in your market.

Sales Leads

Sales leads take the form of bingo cards in response to advertising and sales promotion programs; referrals from satisfied customers, usually obtained by asking for them; and, on extremely rare occasions, a letter or a telephone call from a prospective customer from out of the blue.

In a start-up situation, sales leads are hard to get and can be very expensive to obtain. They are more plentiful and less expensive to obtain for an ongoing company. Regardless of whether you are a start-up or an ongoing company, consider sales leads as precious things that must be carefully handled and nurtured. To the entrepreneur they have all the qualities of an uncut diamond. Sales leads need to be qualified, assigned to a sales representative, and relentlessly followed up until the customer makes a buying decision.

Qualifying Sales Leads

People respond to advertising and sales promotion programs for various reasons. Some have decided to make a purchase and are collecting up-to-date data on competitive products. Some are considering a future purchase and are collecting product data to determine how much to budget for the purchase. Others, for reasons best known to them, enjoy collecting product literature but never intend to buy anything. College students are notorious literature collectors.

The qualification process is usually a telephone conversation with the prospect. If the prospect turns out to be a literature collector, thank the prospect for showing interest in your product and discard the sales lead. If the prospect turns out to be a potential customer, gather as much data as possible on the anticipated timing of the purchase and note the actions you think necessary to convert the prospect to one of your customers. In a start-up situation, it is recommended that you or one of your partners qualify sales leads in the home office before they are assigned to sales representatives. In an ongoing situation, you should determine which of your various sales representatives will qualify and diligently pursue sales leads of their own volition and which require leads to be prequalified before they will pursue them.

Sales Lead Follow-Up

Create a sales lead follow-up file for each of your sales representatives. When you assign a sales lead, establish a time limit by which the sales representative will have called on the customer to start the closing process. It is recommended that you establish a pattern of weekly follow-up by phone or in person to determine the progress or lack thereof each sales representative is making in the closing process for each sales lead assigned. Once you have established a steady follow-up pattern with your sales representatives, they will follow up with the customer because they know you are going to follow them up. Make it clear at the outset that you expect and demand that your representatives diligently follow up each precious, expensive sales lead you provide.

It is recommended that either you or your sales representative follow up periodically with users of your product. If there are problems with the product, you will be better off learning about them on a call from you to the customer rather than one from the customer to you. Continuing periodic follow-up with satisfied customers with no problems can also pay your company dividends. Establishing and continuing a rapport with a satisfied customer can provide you with follow-up orders from your existing customers, sales leads, and favorable recommendations to prospective new customers.

Closing Programs

Closing programs are designed to convert sales opportunities in limbo to booked orders. One school of thought is to design closing programs to motivate sales representatives. Another approach is to motivate customers. These suggestions are aimed at motivating customers that are procrastinating in placing their order or are vacillating between your product and a competitive product.

- When you plan a price increase, contact all potential customers, urging them to "place your order now to avoid the scheduled price increase."

- Offer a seasonal limited-time-frame discount on all orders placed within your specified seasonal dates.

- If your product has several added-cost options, offer one of them at no charge for all orders placed by a date you specify.

- If warranty costs seem to be lower than planned, consider offering an extended limited warranty period for all orders placed by the date specified.

- If your terms are F.O.B. your factory, offer to pay the freight on all orders placed by the date specified.

SALES REPRESENTATIVES

Unless you are a mail-order house dealing directly with consumers, you will need some form of field sales representation. Nearly all start-up and small ongoing companies that need sales representation in the field use sales representatives. This discussion of managing a network of field sales representatives is also applicable to managing a cadre of direct field salespeople.

Sources of Sales Representatives

The best source of sales representatives is conversion of those that represent the large company you previously worked for to representing your company. Most trade journals have a classified advertising section that includes a lines wanted category, listing sales representatives that are looking for additional lines to increase their business or to replace lines that they have lost. The more ambitious direct salespeople of large companies selling products similar to yours are good candidates to spin off and start their independent sales representative company, starting, of course, with your product. In this case an advance or draw may be necessary.

Qualifying Sales Representatives

Training someone, say, an engineer or a user, who is familiar with your type of product to sell is a costly and time-consuming process. Training a proven salesperson on your type of product and market is less costly and time-consuming, but not as efficient as finding people familiar with your type of product and market that are proven sales professionals. The qualification process starts with the telephone and culminates with a one-on-one interview.

Allegiance

Sales representatives tend to pledge allegiance to principals that have the easiest product to sell, pay the highest commissions, and have the fewest post-sale customer involvement or product problems. Provide them with support in the form of prompt replies to questions and requests for assistance, and otherwise demonstrate a real interest in them. The care and feeding of your field sales representatives is important. Nurture them.

Performance Measurement

The sales lead and quotation follow-up systems previously discussed provide the wherewithal to measure the performance of your sales representatives in pursuing sales opportunities provided by you or generated by them. It is also recommended that you establish sales goals or quotas with them. Monthly quotas are preferable because they impose the greatest pressure on the representative. Quarterly goals are marginal. Yearly goals are practically worthless.

The real measure of performance is the ratio of booked orders to orders that, in your opinion, should have been booked. If an otherwise successful representative hits a slump, patience is recommended for a reasonable length of time. If a new representative does not get off the ground in what you consider to be a reasonable length of time, provide an ultimatim and commence the search for a replacement.

Commissions

A sales commission usually takes the form of a percentage of the list price of the product, paid by your company to your sales representative when the representative makes a sale.

In a start-up situation, booking orders is of paramount importance. In this case, it is suggested that you pay all or a significant portion of the commission to the representative when the sale is booked. Knowing that the money will be forthcoming within days of mailing you an order is a strong incentive for your representative to concentrate on your product rather than those of other principals.

When you are a more established ongoing company, it is suggested that you change your commission policy and pay the entire commission or a significant portion of it when you receive payment from the customer. This policy will motivate your sales representative to provide whatever post-sale product or customer support is needed to secure payment from your customer.

QUOTATIONS

Quotations can be verbal, handwritten, or typed on a quotation form or a personalized letter. In the case of a verbal quote, document it on paper. If quotations are made from the home office, provide the sales representative responsible for the account with a copy of each quotation. Make sure that you receive a copy of all quotes made by your sales representative. A quotation is a close-in sales lead and goes in your individual sales representative's follow-up file.

Figure 16-24 is an example of a quotation form.

SALES ORDERS

There is no legal requirement that you acknowledge a customer's purchase order with an acknowledgment or a sales order. Some customers will insist on an acknowledgment or your sales order in response to their purchase order. Others will not. A typical sales order form is shown in Figure 16-25.

Whether or not you decide to issue formal sales orders, it is recommended that you establish a sales order numbering system, a sales order log, and a sales order file system from the outset.

Sales Order Numbering System

The sales order number is your internal control number for all the paper used to process the sales order. Sales order numbers are used on the build-ship schedule, time records, special job bills of material and documentation, customer invoices and packing lists, and the sales order file. Start your sales order numbering system with number 1 and proceed in sequentially ascending number order.

Sales Order Log

The sales order log, Figure 16-7, notes your sequentially ascending sales order number, the sales order date, the customer's purchase order number and date, the address of your customer or institution, the customer-institution contact person, and your sales representative. The sales order log serves as a cross-reference document and is used in the recall-retrofit process.

Sales Order File

The sales order file contains the original customer purchase order, a copy of the sales order, a copy of all invoices and debit-credit memos, and copies of all telecon reports and correspondence with the customer. The open sales order file contains all sales orders that have not been completely shipped. When everything is complete, the completed sales order goes in a closed sales order file.

INTERNATIONAL MARKETS

Everything involved in consummating an international sale is similar to but distinctly different from a domestic sale. The balance of this chapter will discuss these differences and suggest methods of coping with them.

Locating International Sales Representatives

The U.S. Department of Commerce has a wealth of data, information, and programs encompassing virtually every type of product and every country dealing with the marketing aspects of international sales. The Department of Commerce is a prime source for locating and, to a limited degree, qualifying foreign sales representatives. Foreign sales representatives tend to be subscribers to U.S. publications covering industries, professions, and associations in their field of interest. Check the lines wanted category of the classified advertising section or place a line offered advertisement yourself.

Sales Promotion

The Department of Commerce offers a number of sales promotion programs which, for practical purposes, tend to turn up potential sales representatives more often than valid sales leads. Part of the qualification process for international sales representatives should be their ability to conceive and conduct sales promotion programs in their territory.

Product

Some modification to your product may be required for international sales. Despite endless international standardization conferences, each country has slightly different standards. Depending on the type and extent of required modifications, you might well consider a policy of providing your product to your international sales representatives "as is" and holding them responsible for modifying the product to conform to local standards or codes.

Quotations

The buyer-seller relationship in international sales tends to be quite formal and structured. In addition to a formal quotation or proposal, a pro forma invoice is often required. A pro forma invoice is an invoice prepared in your normal fashion with the words "pro forma" noted at the top. Take care in preparing it. Your final actual invoice is expected to be an exact duplicate of the pro forma invoice.

International quotations and pro forma invoices should make it crystal clear that F.O.B. is your dock; the cost of export packaging and packing is to be borne by the buyer; all customs, broker's, or other fees are the responsibility of the buyer; and the transaction is based on U.S. dollars.

Shipping Documents

Documents such as customs declarations and customs invoices are often required over and above your normal invoice and packing list. Customs brokers or freight forwarders will provide all the necessary forms and will assist you in preparing them completely and correctly. These people make their living by providing everything that is needed to move the product from your dock to the customer's facility. You can locate them in the Yellow Pages.

Packaging and Packing

Your customs broker or freight forwarder can advise you on the precise packaging and packing requirements for each international sales order. Packaging and packing requirements for overseas shipments include what is necessary for the product to survive international shipment and will also include specifications or standards peculiar to the destination country. It is recommended that you determine packaging and packing requirements before you make a quotation or submit a pro forma invoice so that the charges will be included on your quotation and pro forma invoice.

Payment Terms

Most larger commercial banks have a person or a department that can assist you in the financial aspects of international sales. It is recommended that your payment terms for international sales be on a letter-of-credit basis. A letter-of-credit transaction is similar to an escrow transaction. The conditions of a letter of credit are negotiated prior to the sale and should be included on your quotation, the pro forma invoice, the customer's purchase order, and your sales order. The customer condition is that the customer is to remit the total value of the transaction in U.S. dollars when you have fulfilled your condition. Your condition is related to shipment of the product. It can be when you turn the shipment over to the forwarder, when the shipment has landed in the customer's country, when the shipment has cleared your customer's country's customs, or some specified period of time after the shipment has cleared customs. It is recommended you do not agree to anything beyond the foregoing.

The mechanics of a letter-of-credit transaction are quite simple. After the order is booked and acknowledged by your sales order, your customer deposits the U.S. dollar value of the transaction in a bank. When your customer's bank receives the U.S. dollar value of the transaction from your customer, it writes the letter of credit specifying the conditions to your bank and provides a copy to you and to your customs broker or forwarder. When your customs broker or forwarder has fulfilled your condition, they provide certified documentation to that effect to your bank, which in turn provides it to your customer's bank. Your customer's bank then forwards the funds to your bank. When your bank receives the funds, it authorizes the broker or forwarder to release the shipment to your customer and remit the funds to you.

Post-Sale Product and Customer Support

One of the key factors in qualifying international sales representatives is their ability to provide everything that is needed in the way of post-sale support for the product and the customer. Your involvement should be limited to providing documentation or advice by telephone.

5

POST-SALE
SUPPORT AND
PRODUCT LIABILITY

Some level of post-sale support is demanded by the marketplace and is also a statutory requirement under federal and state laws called uniform commercial codes. The laws of the land also hold you and your company liable and responsible for personal injury and property damage caused by your product.

Product liability considerations and your post-sale support-level policies are becoming increasingly important. Customers as individuals or groups (so-called class actions) and government agencies (federal, state, county, and local) are becoming more vocal, strident, and powerful. The courts, as evidenced by increasingly higher premiums for product liability insurance, are also becoming more consumer- and less manufacturer-oriented.

The degree of product liability risk and the post-sale support level are functions of the type of product and its application. Consumable products such as disposable diapers, freezer bags, or light bulbs must function only as advertised and not physically harm the customer. Inanimate products such as furniture or plastic ice-cube trays, although they have a longer life span, only need to be delivered to the customer undamaged, function as intended, and not harm the customer.

Active products with moving parts or active fluid or electric circuitry not only must reach the customer undamaged and function as intended, but may also require on-site installation by professionals, customer training, and continuing maintenance or service support. Active products are inherently more likely to harm or injure customers or others.

This chapter explores ways and means of coping with product liability and post-sale support for all types of products and on-site support for products that require it. Repair-exchange and serial-number systems are also discussed.

PRODUCT LIABILITY

The words "product liability" mean that your company is liable and responsible if your product harms or injures someone. The someone can be your customer or a seemingly uninvolved bystander. You are also liable and responsible for property damage caused by your product.

The extent or degree of product liability risk is a function of the product and its application. Potential product liability for a life-support system in an intensive care ward is about as high-risk as you can get. A plastic ice-cube tray is at the other end of the risk spectrum.

Product Liability Insurance

There are a limited number of insurance companies or carriers that write product liability insurance. Your insurance broker can put you in touch with carriers in your area offering product liability insurance. Product liability insurance can be expensive, so shop several carriers. The carriers will send a product liability expert to your facility to learn in detail what your product is, what it does, and its application. Based on this appraisal, they will quote you the premium for product liability insurance.

Whether or not you decide to carry product liability insurance is dependent on two factors: Must you have it and can you afford it? If your customers demand that you have product liability insurance, you must carry it or they will buy from a competitor who does. If your customers do not demand that you carry product liability insurance, you should still consider adding it to your total insurance package. Without coverage, a product liability action against your product could well sink your company and you. If you cannot afford it and your customers don't demand it, proceed without it.

The decision to forgo product liability insurance should not be taken lightly. Hardly a week goes by without, from the viewpoint of the manufacturer, a horror story being reported on a product liability case. Assuming that you have product liability insurance, if your customer requires proof that you are covered, your insurance carrier will, at your request and at no charge, provide your customer with a certificate to that effect.

If you have a high-risk product, you can ask for and receive product liability certificates of coverage from vendors of key parts or materials the failure of which may be the reason for a product liability action against your company. From a potential product liability standpoint, purchasing key parts or material from vendors who carry product liability insurance spreads the risk and may earn you lower premiums. Vendors that carry product liability insurance do not charge more than those without it.

Recall-Retrofit

A product *recall* is repossession of a defective product with replacement or refund of the purchase price to the customer.

A *retrofit* is similar to a recall but applies to a defective product that is permanently installed or otherwise physically incapable of being removed from the customer, such as an automobile hoist permanently installed in the floor of a garage. A retrofit also applies when the customer or a local repair facility can repair the defect using replacement parts or materials and instructions provided by you.

Recalls or retrofits can be either voluntary or involuntary and usually occur when a defective product can or may cause physical injury. You may decide on a recall or retrofit for some other reason, but potential physical harm is normally the trigger to invoke a product recall or retrofit.

A voluntary recall-retrofit is one you instigate. An involuntary recall-retrofit occurs when a federal agency learns of a potentially dangerous situation and requests the manufacturer to invoke a recall-retrofit, and the manufacturer refuses to do so. In this case the federal agency can force, via their statutory authority and the courts, an involuntary recall.

Some of the federal agencies with recall-retrofit jurisdiction include:

- The Consumer Product Safety Commission

- The Federal Trade Commission

- The Food and Drug Administration

- The National Highway Safety Administration

If you discover that a defective product which could potentially cause physical harm or injury is in your distribution system or in your customers' hands, you should seriously consider some level of voluntary recall-retrofit. Recalls or retrofits are expensive, but so are personal injury or property damage lawsuits. Additionally, if a federal agency invokes an involuntary recall-retrofit on your company, they will also seek to have a substantial fine levied against your company. Get your attorney or legal counsel on board before you initiate a recall or retrofit.

The laws under which various federal government agencies with recall-retrofit jurisdiction operate usually require the manufacturer to contact the agency prior to commencing a recall-retrofit. It is recommended that you do so. Their interest in a recall-retrofit situation is the same as yours . . . to prevent, if at all possible, injury caused by a defective product.

The first step is to determine, in concert with the appropriate federal agency, the severity of the problem. Recalls and retrofits are generally classified as class 1 or class 2 depending on the nature and severity of the condition requiring correction:

- Class 1—A condition exists such that the product should cease to be used until the condition has been corrected or the defective product replaced because of a high probability of personal injury.

- Class 2—A condition exists that must be corrected, but the product may continue to be used under specified restrictions invoked by you on the user to preclude personal injury.

The next step is to spread the word to your customers. In the case of a mass-distribution product, the federal agency can be very helpful in assisting in the preparation of a press release. They are also influential with the wire services and other media in getting the release published.

For products requiring on-site installation and continuing maintenance or service, the federal agency will probably require you to contact each customer individually. In this case, the invoice log or the sales order log is the database for initiating a recall or retrofit.

The federal agency will probably require you to keep records and provide them with periodic reports noting such things as the quantity of product recalled, timing of completion for products requiring on-site retrofit, and corrective actions taken to preclude future problems.

POST-SALE SUPPORT

Your post-sale support level, let's call it the support level, is a combination of policies and programs that provide post-sale support to the product, the customer, or both.

Uniform commercial codes notwithstanding, there are probably historical imperatives in your industry that will spell out the minimum level of support you must provide to remain competitive.

Support-level considerations for consumable and inanimate products are relatively simple and straightforward: post-sale support is limited to repair or replacement of defective products under the terms delineated in your limited warranty.

In the case of active products with moving parts or active fluid or electric circuitry, the support level can be a significant cost factor. The lower the support level, the lower the cost of the program. On the other hand, a support level significantly and measurably more generous that that of your competitors, properly exploited, can become a good marketing tool.

One way to get at a support level that makes sense for your product and your company is to put yourself in your customer's moccasins and look at your product, your company, and your competitors from that viewpoint. . . . The minimum support level will probably equate closely to the industry average or norm: higher on some factors, lower on other factors, but, on balance, normal or average for the industry. The maximum level is probably a composite of the most generous level offered for each factor by all significant competitors in the industry.

What your actual support level turns out to be will probably be your intuitive feel for what you can afford to invest over and above the minimum as a tradeoff for increased sales at the expense of your less generous competitors. Over time, support levels in a given industry tend to rise. More reliable circuit design and components have stretched warranty periods for television sets up to 4 calendar years. Better materials and manufacturing methods have increased automobile drive train warranties to as high as 50,000 miles. If you have a high level of confidence in your product, why not opt for a higher support level than your competition and enjoy a market advantage, albeit probably short.

Uniform Commercial Code

Uniform commercial codes are laws that define the minimum you must meet or exceed with your post-sale support-level policy and program. To be competitive in your industry, your support level will probably exceed uniform commercial code minimums. There is a federal uniform commercial code. Some states have also enacted uniform commercial codes; these are usually more stringent than the federal statute. Your attorney can tell you whatever you need to know about uniform commercial codes.

Limited Warranty

It is recommended that you draft your limited warranty statement in concert with legal counsel.

Let's discuss the term "limited warranty." What it means is that your warranty is limited by the conditions spelled out in your limited warranty statement. The primary purpose of the limited warranty is to limit your liability or responsibility to cover only the repair or replacement of defective product and avoid any responsibility for anything other than repair or replacement. To accomplish this objective, limited warranties usually conclude with a sentence to this effect: "There is no other express warranty on goods covered by this agreement."

Limited warranties usually start out with a sentence to this effect: "The seller warrants that all new products of its manufacture shall be free from defects in material and workmanship under normal use and service." From this point on, limited warranties vary depending on the post-sale support-level policy of the individual company. Limited warranty variables include the time period, whether the defective product is repaired or replaced, and who pays transportation to and from the customer and the repair site.

It is also possible to impose conditions of use on the customer the violation of which will void the limited warranty, such as minimum and maximum environmental conditions for operation and storage of the product and whether the product must be repaired by a manufacturer-designated service representative or whether customers may effect their own repair. The warranty period for a chain saw used by a lumberjack should be shorter than that for one used by the owner of one small wood-burning stove.

Although they may not do it, your customers should be given the opportunity to read your limited warranty statement prior to their decision to purchase your product. This is necessary to avoid disagreement on what your limited warranty specifically does and does not cover. Products that are marketed in a packaged condition in a retail outlet usually have the warranty statement printed on the package. Products that are displayed outside of their package in a retail outlet usually have the warranty statement on the tag or brochure attached to the product that extols its virtues. Products that are shipped to the customer from the factory usually have the warranty statement in the catalog, brochure, quotation, and sales order.

Warranty Reserve

One of the prime considerations in determining your support level and delineating it in your limited warranty statement is its cost, either in dollars per unit or as a percentage of sales. For purposes of discussion, let's assume that you estimate your warranty cost at 5 percent of sales. Whether in practice it turns out to be exactly 5 percent, 1 percent, or 10 percent is not germane to this discussion of warranty reserve. You will cover warranty costs out of current cash, and this will be recorded as an expense against profit. It may appear that the simplest way to handle warranty expense is to period-cost it. Under this procedure, whatever warranty expense you incur in an accounting period is period-costed during that accounting period. In a start-up situation, period-costing warranty expense is perfectly acceptable. However, when you need or are required to provide certified financial statements, the public accounting firm certifying your statements will insist on a warranty reserve. An entity called the Financial Accounting Standards Board (FASB) has established accounting rules that must be followed by accredited certified public accounting firms. An FASB rule requires a warranty reserve if a company incurs warranty expense.

Let's assume that your estimated or experienced warranty is, indeed, 5 percent of sales. You establish the warranty reserve by expensing 5 percent of sales against profit and crediting 5 percent of sales to a warranty reserve each month. As warranty expense is incurred, it is charged against the warranty reserve rather than being period-costed against profit in the month incurred.

The theory behind a warranty reserve is that the day you ship a product, you have incurred a liability equal to 5 percent of the selling price of that product. The reserve provides the wherewithal to honor that warranty liability even if, for whatever reason, you cease operation and go out of business.

Once again, period-costing warranty expense is perfectly acceptable in the start-up situation. Bear in mind, however, that with the advent of certified financial statements, a warranty reserve of fairly sizable proportion will come out of profit in the year you become certified.

ON-SITE SUPPORT

Post-sale support of products that must be performed on site at the customer's facility can be a significant cost factor and time-consuming. On-site support can include customer training, product maintenance service, or both.

Customer Training

Most customers have a natural aversion to reading even the best written operating manual. Hands-on training of customers using your product in their application seems to produce the best and most lasting results.

Some, but not all, service representatives are capable of customer training. Most sales representatives make good trainers . . . they actually commence the training program during the selling process.

Assuming that your training program does not require a several-day or week course for the customer in your training facility, it is recommended that the qualification and selection process for sales representatives and service representatives include their ability to provide customer training as part of your arrangement with them.

As with on-site installation training of service representatives, to be discussed later, it is recommended that you conduct one or several customer training programs on site at the customer's facility in concert with either your sales or service representative. Once they have gone through several hands-on training sessions with you, they should be able to handle future customer training without your direct support.

Field Service Representatives

If you are a spin-off from a large company and are planning a product similar to that of your former company, you probably know who their service people are in various cities or locations. In this case, service people employed by your former company represent a trained cadre of potential moonlighters that will probably enjoy the extra income derived from servicing your products.

If your product is different from what you were used to with your former company, you will undoubtedly know what major companies produce a product similar to yours. Walking through the Yellow Pages of cities or locations where you anticipate you will need a service capability can easily provide you with the telephone numbers of the service offices of those larger companies. Further perusal of the Yellow Pages should disclose independent service companies that appear, from their names or advertisements, to service your type of product. Public libraries usually have telephone directories for major cities in their reference sections.

The first step in the qualification process is a phone call and a discussion of the service representative's experience and apparent skill level as it relates to your needs. When you visit the city or location of a prospective service resource, you can conduct a face-to-face interview.

The extent of the training your cadre of field service representatives requires will, of course, depend on their skill level, their related experience, and the complexities of your product. One method that is quite successful is to travel to the location for the first and possibly additional installations and train the field service representative on site or at their office prior to the installation at the customer's facility. Nothing beats hands-on training.

The maximum you should have to pay your field service representatives for installation and warranty service calls is the going rate they charge their customers if they are an independent service company. You should be able to negotiate a lower rate than they currently charge their customers. They do not incur any sales expense to add your product and customers to their service base. They negotiate and secure service contracts after the warranty period expires. In the case of moonlighters employed by a larger company, you should be able to hire them at something less than their current salary.

Installation, Warranty Service

In the start-up situation, installation and warranty service costs, of necessity, are your best estimate. It is suggested that your estimates be on the conservative side. "Murphy's law" will probably prevail. An account should be set up for installation costs, and they should be period-costed. Installation is normally accomplished in the same accounting period as shipment or in the succeeding period. Therefore an installation reserve account is not needed and is not recommended. Warranty expense, as previously discussed, can be either period-costed or washed through a warranty reserve account.

Actual experienced costs for installation and warranty are accumulated in their expense accounts. This historical cost data, usually looked at as a ratio or percentage of sales, is used in future price adjustment considerations for ongoing products and as a factor in the financial evaluation of new product projects.

Contract Service, Paid Service

Post-warranty service is normally provided by your service professional on either a service contract or paid service call basis. Service contracts usually cover a 1-year time period. In return for purchasing a service contract, the customer receives all required service during the period covered by the contract at no additional charge. A rule-of-thumb price for a 1-year service contract is 18 percent of the product selling price. Paid service calls are just that. A customer who needs the product serviced pays the going rate for time and materials expended in performing the required service.

It is recommended that your service policy with your service representatives enables you to get out of the service loop when the warranty period has ended. Staying in the loop by having service contracts between your company and the customer or invoices for paid service calls coming from you to the customer will lead to a lot of paper shuffling on your part with little, if any, income resulting from it. The bread and butter of an independent local service company is an ever-expanding customer base of service contracts or arrangements for paid service calls. So let them shuffle the service paper and devote your time to selling new customers.

As far as your customer is concerned, your service-level policy is spelled out in your limited warranty statement. But you also need a policy for your field service representatives: insist that your service representatives provide you with useful service call reports before you pay them for service calls. If a report, "It did not work and I fixed it" is satisfactory to you, so be it. On the other hand, the causes of failures, learned from service reports, are valuable data for correcting design deficiencies.

REPAIR-EXCHANGE

Repair-exchange items, sometimes called factory rebuilts, are a time-honored program that customers think saves them money and that can be a significant source of profit or income for you. Generally speaking, repair-exchange items are priced at about 60 percent of the price of a new item. The 40 percent saving is significant in the customer's eyes. You get the defective item for nothing, and it if is just a matter of replacing an O ring or a resistor, you will end up making more on repair-exchange items than you do on new products.

Although repair-exchange items are used for in-warranty repair, repair-exchange programs become effective after the expiration of the warranty. You will need, as discussed in Chapter 4, "Marketing," a price list for new items and repair-exchange items as well as for spare parts. The sale of new items or spare parts is straightforward. A repair-exchange program requires a repair-exchange policy and a paperwork system.

A suggested repair-exchange policy should include the following:

- Units that are available as repair-exchange

- The defective unit returned to the factory under a repair-exchange transaction must be repairable or the customer must pay the price for a new unit.

- Repair-exchange units should have the same limited warranty coverage as new units.

The paperwork system for a repair-exchange program is covered on the repair-exchange flowchart, Figure 5-1, and involves a repair-exchange work order, Figure 16-29.

Following the flowchart, on receipt of a repair-exchange purchase order

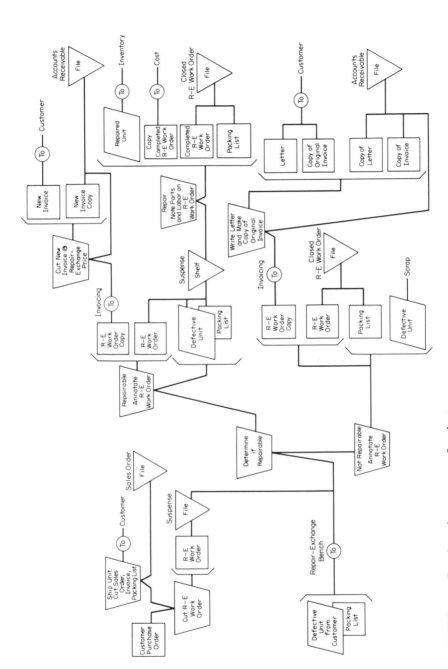

FIGURE 5-1 Repair-exchange system flowchart

from the customer, cut a sales order and invoice, at the new unit price, and packing list set, with the following annotation on the invoice and a similar statement on the sales order: "This invoice covers shipment of a replacement part number _____ against your purchase order number _____. The defective unit is to be returned, transportation paid, to *(your company)*. On examination, a new invoice in the amount of $*(repair-exchange price)* will be issued if the returned defective unit is repairable. If the returned defective unit is not repairable, notice will be forwarded to pay this invoice." Ship the repair-exchange unit to the customer. (Your first repair-exchange unit shipped will probably be a new one.)

Cut a repair-exchange (R-E) work order, Figure 16-29, noting the part number, revision, description, customer, customer purchase order, and service representative. Put the R-E work order in a suspense file. Keep track of R-E work orders with a repair-exchange work order log, Figure 16-30.

Upon receipt of the defective unit from the customer, forward it and the packing list to the repair-exchange bench for a determination of its repairability. If it is repairable, so note on the R-E work order and forward a copy of the R-E work order to invoicing.

Invoicing cuts a new invoice at the repair-exchange price and forwards the invoice to the customer for payment. The invoice is annotated: "The defective part number _____ returned to *(your company)* against your purchase order _____ has been found repairable. Accordingly, please destroy invoice number _____ dated _____ and process this invoice for payment."

The defective unit, the packing list, and the R-E work order are then placed in a repair-exchange unit suspense shelf to await repair. Repair of repair-exchange units, unless they get repaired in the process of determining if they are repairable, is normally accomplished as fill-in work. It is suggested that no value be assigned to repair-exchange inventory. Ultimately, repair-exchange inventory will cease to move and will become obsolete. It is better not to value it to avoid an inventory writeoff against profit in the future when it becomes obsolete and is scrapped. When the unit is repaired, note the labor hours and parts and material used on the R-E work order and forward a copy of the complete R-E work order to cost. Keep the R-E work order and packing list in a closed R-E work order file as an audit trail. Tag the repaired unit as having been repaired and tested and place it in repair-exchange inventory.

If the defective unit is deemed not repairable, so note on the R-E work order and forward a copy to invoicing. Invoicing sends a letter to the customer covering the following: "The defective part number _____ returned under your purchase order _____ has been found not repairable. Accordingly, please process our invoice number _____ dated _____, copy attached, for prompt payment."

Scrap the defective unit after salvaging any reusable parts. Place the closed R-E work order and the packing list in a closed R-E work order file as an audit trail.

It is suggested that a repair-exchange account be established to record sales revenue and repair costs from repair-exchange transactions. Credit this account with invoices at the repair-exchange price. (If the new unit price prevails because the defective returned unit was not repairable, that sale should be booked against a spare parts revenue account.) Debit the repair-exchange account with all parts, material, and labor charges accumulated against R-E work orders as defective units are repaired. This account, noting repair-exchange revenue and expense, provides data on the profitability or lack thereof of the repair-exchange program for future repair-exchange pricing decisions.

SERIAL-NUMBER SYSTEM

Unless there is some compelling reason, such as an edict from a regulatory agency or some other internal imperative, do not fuss with serial numbers. They are to be avoided if at all possible. In practice, keeping track of serialized units is a complex and time-consuming process. It often ends up as an exercise in futility unless a highly disciplined system is rigorously enforced.

In the event that a serial-number system is required but only for the total finished product, you will need serial-number name plates and a serial-number log, Figure 16-31, to keep track of them.

In the event that subassemblies, in addition to the finished product, also require serial numbers, each item, whether it is a finished product or a subassembly, requiring a serial number will have a discrete part number. A serial-number log is needed for each discrete part number that is to be serial-numbered. Additionally, you will need a "parent" file for each finished product shipped noting what serialized subassemblies were shipped with it.

If a serialized subassembly is replaced by a different serialized subassembly, the following transactions are required:

- Post the replacement unit to the finished product parent file.

- Post the replaced unit off the parent file and note where it went as an audit trail.

- Post the replacement unit to the appropriate serial-number log.

- Post the new location of the replaced unit to its serial-number log. For example, if the replaced unit was scrapped, post it as scrapped. If it ends up in repair-exchange inventory, post it to repair-exchange inventory. When it is shipped and installed in another finished product, repeat all the above.

The simplest, most straightforward serial-number system is to start with number 1 and proceed in ascending sequence.

PART THREE
THE START-UP MANUFACTURING SYSTEM

Most start-up manufacturing companies commence operations with a single product or a limited product line that has few, if any, options. Start-up companies also tend to have limited resources: either just the entrepreneur or very few partners, and a tight supply of cash. The start-up manufacturing systems discussed in Chapter 6 are aimed at conserving cash and making as much entrepreneur time as possible available for developing the product and getting it to the marketplace.

CHAPTER 6: START-UP MANUFACTURING PROCESS

This chapter describes a method of subcontracting the entire manufacturing function and a bare-bones system for in-house manufacturing that is adequate for the company with a single product or a modest product line.

6
START-UP MANUFACTURING PROCESS

This chapter starts with the premise that an engineering model or a prototype of your first product exists, that it works, and that you have determined the quantity to be manufactured in the first production lot. The paperwork necessary to commence manufacturing includes two database documents and seven working documents.

The needed database documents are the bill of material and engineering drawings, Figures 15-2 and 15-3. If you have already created parts lists noting the quantity of each piece part, assembly, and material item required to make the product, label them "bill of material" and assign part numbers to them. If you do not have parts lists, create them using the bill of material format. If you have sketches of each unique piece part, label them "engineering drawings" and assign part numbers to them. If you do not have sketches or drawings, create them using the engineering drawing format. Make sure that your bills of material and drawings completely define the product so that it can be manufactured.

The seven working documents you will need are the purchase order, purchase order log, commitment log, invoice, packing list, invoice log, and sales order log, Figures 16-1 through 16-7. Working documents are action documents that keep track of parts, material, assemblies, and labor as the manufacturing process is accomplished.

MAKE OR BUY

One of the first major decisions in any manufacturing process is which parts and assemblies to make and which to buy. By definition, all material items and standard catalog parts are purchased. Make-or-buy decisions are needed for those piece parts and assemblies that are unique to your product. Normally, the key factor in the make-or-buy decision is cost. In a start-up situation, the key decision factor should be: Can it be purchased or must we make it? If unique parts and assemblies can be purchased with reasonable assurance that their quality will be satisfactory and if the cost to purchase them is not exorbitant, you will be wise to decide to purchase. Making something in-house requires management time and cash to obtain and set up the equipment needed to fabricate it, create the manufacturing process, hire and train the production workers, and continue to supervise production. In a start-up situation you will be wise to buy as much as you possibly can and limit manufacturing to operations that, for whatever reason, can only be performed in-house. Not only will this policy conserve cash, it will, importantly, provide more precious entrepreneur time for attending to the marketplace and getting the product to it.

One company the author has worked with purchases their product complete from a subcontractor. They provide the subcontractor with a single purchase order, a set of documentation, and a model. When the subcontractor has all parts and material on hand ready to assemble, one of the partners spends a day at the subcontractor's facility training the subcontractor's work force in the subtle nuances of the product. The subcontractor carries all inventory and invoices the company, with 30-day payment terms, when delivery is made. The company tailors each unit of product to its specific customer application and performs the final pre-shipment test. The company's payment terms to their customer are net on delivery. More times than not, they deliver the product and collect their money before they pay their subcontractor. Management time spent on manufacturing is limited to the 1 or 2 days needed to negotiate price and delivery and to train the subcontractor's work force. Cash flow is as good as it is possible to achieve.

COMPLETE SUBCONTRACTING

There are companies that specialize in manufacturing other companies' products. These companies, let's call them complete subcontractors, operate in different ways. Some will purchase all parts and material, fabricate unique parts, assemble, test, package, and pack the product for shipment, and drop-ship to your customer when you provide them with a packing list and shipping label. Some will carry parts and material, work in process, and finished goods inventory and will invoice you when they ship to your customer. Others will carry parts, material, and work in process and will invoice you as units are placed in finished goods. Others will want progress payments.

It is recommended that you consider a complete subcontractor to avoid investing precious entrepreneur time and cash in setting up and managing an in-house manufacturing capability, and that you negotiate as strongly as possible to defer payment as long as possible. Subcontractors that will defer payment will probably add an administrative cost to cover their cost of money, but this will not greatly exceed, if at all, what you would pay for money if you manufactured the product in-house. Subcontractors obviously make a profit, but they tend to be quite economical and competitive. Their bread and butter is manufacturing your product as well as you could for not much more than it would cost you.

IN-HOUSE MANUFACTURING

Complete subcontracting may not be feasible or desirable. The simplest, most straightforward, and most practical in-house manufacturing system for a start-up situation is called *job lot*. You decide how many end product units to manufacture in a job or lot. You purchase or fabricate the job-lot quantities of each purchased material item, standard catalog part, unique piece part, and assembly; when they are all available, you assemble them in one single job lot into the final product. Figure 6-1, the start-up manufacturing system flowchart, illustrates the job-lot system.

Let's assume that you have decided to manufacture 50 of your model ABC in your first production lot. The lot number will be ABC-001. The second production lot number for model ABC will be ABC-002; the third, ABC-003, and so on. It is common practice to identify production lots with the part number and a sequentially ascending lot number. The part number facilitates identification; the lot number keeps track of each lot. It is not unusual to have several lots in process at the same time for the same part number.

Following the flowchart, the first step is to generate requirements for all purchased material items, purchased standard catalog parts, unique piece parts, and assemblies. The top-level model ABC bill of material is the tool used to generate requirements: Theoretically, ordering fifty sets of everything on the top-level ABC bill of material should do it. Fifty sets of most parts will probably do it. Some parts will end up as scrap in your assembly and test process or will be prone to failure in the field, and you will have to replace them. Apply your best judgment and wisdom and determine how many of what part numbers should be ordered in excess of fifty sets.

Purchased Material Items   Use a separate purchase order form for each vendor. You will need to order somewhat more than fifty times the gross material required for each model ABC to cover anticipated normal scrap. Note ABC-001 on each purchase order form as an audit trail.

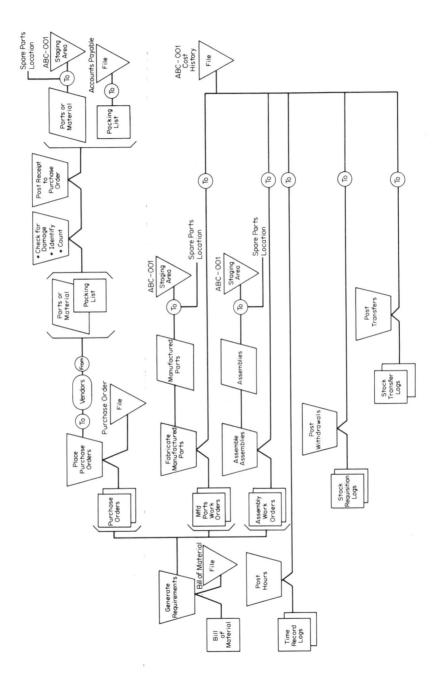

FIGURE 6-1 Start-up manufacturing-company system flowchart

Purchased Standard Catalog Parts   Use a separate purchase order form for each vendor and your best judgment of how many more than fifty sets to order. Note ABC-001 on each purchase order form as an audit trail.

Manufactured Parts   If you have the equivalent of production route sheets, Figure 15-8, use a copy as the manufactured-part work order. If not, use a copy of the part drawing. Note lot 001 and the quantity on the route sheets or drawings to constitute manufactured-part work orders.

Assemblies   Use a copy of each bill of material or parts list as the work order for assemblies. Noting lot 001 and the quantity on bills of material constitutes assembly work orders.

The next step is to place the purchase orders, fabricate manufactured parts, and assemble assemblies.

Place Purchase Orders   If you can afford the time to secure competitive quotations for purchased material items and standard catalog parts, and feel you can save money by doing so, shop several vendors you are confident with, by telephone, and place the order by phone with the low bidder. Written purchase orders are not necessary. Most vendors will accept a phone order. In the case of a sole-source vendor, make your place-the-order call sound like you are shopping; and, when you place the order, make it sound like that vendor did provide the best price.

Figure 6-2 is an example of a purchase order for twenty widgets. The quantity, commodity, and requested delivery are filled in when requirements are generated. The other data are filled in when the order is placed. Be sure you ask for and receive a firm delivery promise. When the order is placed, place it in an open purchase order file.

A word about sales tax: most states require vendors to collect sales tax on sales they make to customers within the same state unless the commodity is for resale to another customer. Normally, if you purchase from a vendor in another state, you will not be involved with sales tax.

If a commodity or service is used to produce your product or becomes part of your product, it is considered for resale. Your state tax people will issue you a resale number to include in your for resale statement on the purchase order, which lets your vendor off the hook. Your certified public accountant can help you obtain the resale number. For commodities or services you purchase that are not destined to become part of your prod-

Purchase Order						

Vendor: *PEERLESS*   P.O. #: *123*

JOE 123 - 4567   Date *1-2-81*

Terms: *NET 30*	F.O.B. *AKRON*	Re-Sale	X	Ship Via: *UPS*		
		Taxable				
Item	Quantity	Commodity	Price	Per	Extension	
	20	*Widgets*	*1 20*	*Ea.*	*24.00*	
				Total	*24.00*	

If re-sale checked above, all items on this order are for re-sale # *123-456-78*	Requested Delivery: *1-15-80*	Promised Delivery *1-22-80*
Requisitioned by: *SRH* Date: *12-30-79*	*YOUR COMPANY*	
Approved: *SDC* Date *12/31/79*		
Phone ☑ Written ☐	By: *DG*	

FIGURE 6-2   Purchase order

uct, such as cleaning supplies, office supplies, and the like, sales tax will be added to the purchase price.

Assign purchase order numbers in sequentially ascending order, using the purchase order log, Figure 16-2, to record numbers that you have assigned and used.

It is recommended that you record all purchases on the commitment log, Figure 16-3. Note the rounded-off dollar total of each order placed in the month you anticipate paying the vendor. You will find the commitment log to be a valuable tool in assessing future cash needs.

When parts or material are received, check the container for obvious damage. If the container is damaged, open it to ascertain whether the contents are damaged. Remember, if the shipment is F.O.B. the vendor's factory, you are responsible for collecting shipping damage claims. Shipping damage claims are covered in Chapter 10, "Receiving."

Assuming that there is no damage to the contents, check that the parts or material are what was ordered, and verify the count as noted on the packing list. If the quantity exceeds that ordered, decide whether to accept the overage or return it to the vendor. If you decide to return the overage, contact the vendor by phone to determine how they want you to return ship the overage. If the amount is less than you ordered, carefully check the packing list (or the invoice when it is received) to make sure that the balance is back-ordered. If a back-order quantity is noted on the packing list or the invoice, call the vendor to determine when the balance will be shipped. If the packing list or invoice is marked to the effect that the order is complete, generate a new requirement and place another order for the balance you need. It is relatively common practice in industry that shipments of $\pm 10\%$ of the purchase order quantity are considered complete.

When the count verification process is complete, post the quantity received on the open purchase order, put the packing list in the accounts payable suspense file, and put the quantity of material or parts needed for lot 001 in a staging area and the spare parts in a spare parts location. When the vendor invoice is received, staple the packing list to it and put them both in an accounts payable suspense file. Accounts payable is covered in Chapter 12.

Fabricate Manufactured Parts   In a start-up situation, manufactured-part work orders tend to be worked when the material is received. Subassembly parts should be completed before final assembly parts. When you decide to work a manufactured-part work order, provide the worker with the work order, material, tools, and instructions on how to do it.

Assembly Work Orders   Subassembly work orders should be completed in the order in which they are needed—the lowest level first, then the next level, and so on. When you decide to work an assembly work order, provide the assembler with the work order, the kit of parts, and instructions on how to do it.

Time Record Logs

Set up a time record for each person in your work force and carefully instruct them to record all their time on the time record to the closest 0.1 hour. Where the time was spent is noted in the work order column. If they are working on assembling lot 001 of model ABC, they would record ABC-001, as shown in Figure 6-3.

If they perform other duties, have them note what they did: pick up, deliver, clean up, etc. You will use these time records to see what your actual model ABC labor amounts to and how much work-force time is spent on extraneous chores. Time records are also an audit trail for your certified public accountant and the Internal Revenue Service.

Staging Area

You will need a staging area and a spare parts location. The staging area and spare parts location can be on the floor, tables or benches, or shelves. Parts and material in a staging area are assigned to assembly work orders and should leave the staging area only as part of an assembly work order kit to be assembled. If staging area parts are needed for some other use, such as spare parts, they should be transferred via a stock transfer form, Figure 6-4.

A stock transfer form, Figure 6-4, is annotated when a model ABC is completed and placed in finished goods or shipped against a customer

Name Joe Smith		Time Record Log			Sheet 1 of 1
Date	Hours	Work Order #	Date	Hours	Work Order #
2-1	8.0	ABC-001			

FIGURE 6-3   Time record log

FEB		Stock Transfer Log				Sheet _1_ of _1_		
Part #	Quantity	Transfer		Cost		Post		
		From	To	Each	Extended	Cost	Inventory	
A B C	2	WIP	STOCK					

FIGURE 6-4   Stock transfer log

order. It is also annotated when parts are transferred from a manufactured-part work order to the staging area or spare parts location, from lower-level assemblies to higher-level assemblies, or from the staging area to a spare parts or other location. If you transfer staging area parts to another location or use, be sure to order a replacement quantity to ensure that you have all the parts required for the final product.

Spare Parts Location

Spare parts placed in a spare parts location are to cover scrap generated in the assembly and test process and to replace field failures. The stock requisition log is annotated when a spare part is applied to a work order, as shown in Figure 6-5. The original fifty sets of parts were charged to lot ABC-001 via the assembly work order. Any spare parts used over and above the original quantity of fifty are charged to lot ABC-001 via the stock requisition log. Spare parts sent to the field as replacements are also charged out on the stock requisition log.

Cost History File

As time records, stock requisitions, and stock transfer forms are filled up, place them in an ABC-001 cost history file. When manufactured-part and

FEB.		Stock Requisition Log				Sheet _1_ of _1_	
Part #	Quantity	Used For		Cost		Post	
		Product	Reason	Each	Extended	Cost	Inventory
X Y Z	2	ABC 001	scrap				

FIGURE 6-5   Stock requisition log

assembly work orders are completed, place them in the ABC-001 cost history file. When the top-level ABC-001 work order is completed, the contents of the ABC-001 cost history file—assembly and manufactured-part work orders, stock requisition logs, stock transfer logs, and time record logs—will contain a complete audit trail of all charges to ABC-001. You can use the cost history file to convert your original cost estimate to an actual cost. Your certified public accountant will use it. The Internal Revenue Service will use it.

Continuing Production

The job-lot manufacturing system is really all you need as long as the product line and the number of options remain modest. Just continue with lot 002, lot 003, and so on. If you have parts and material for more than one top-level production lot in process at the same time, be careful, and discipline your work force to keep the material, parts, assemblies, time charges, stock transfers, and stock requisitions segregated by lot. Misapplication of material or parts will create unplanned and disruptive shortages. Mischarged time, transfers, and requisitions will distort cost history.

As the product line grows and as options are added, the job-lot system will start to cause problems. The job-lot system does not do well with common parts and does not handle different delivery requirements resulting from different lead time setback intervals. When difficulties start to crop up, resist the temptation to use an order-point system. The order-point system, described in detail in Chapter 7, "Material Requirements Planning," consists of establishing minimum-maximum order quantities. When the on-hand balance is reduced to the minimum quantity, an order is automatically placed for the maximum quantity, which, theoretically, should be received before you completely run out of parts or material. On the surface, order-point seems to be the perfect solution. In reality, as discussed in Chapter 7, it is applicable only to inexpensive items with short lead times. Trying to apply it to the mainstream production process will, believe it, only compound your problems, increase shortages, and seriously unbalance inventory—usually to the side of excessive inventory. When you outgrow the job-lot system, a forecast-demand material requirements planning system, described in detail in Chapter 7, is recommended.

The classic symptoms that indicate when to evolve from a job-lot to a forecast-demand material requirements planning system include increased and apparently unexplainable parts shortages and repeat orders for the same part number at very short intervals.

PART FOUR

THE LARGER ONGOING COMPANY MANUFACTURING SYSTEM

This part discusses the more sophisticated systems needed by larger ongoing manufacturing companies with a broad product line with options and a relatively high ratio of common parts and materials.

CHAPTER 7: MATERIAL REQUIREMENTS PLANNING

Chapter 7 describes three methods—job-lot, order-point, and forecast-demand—of determining parts and material requirements: how many of which items are needed on what date.

CHAPTER 8: PURCHASING

This chapter describes a complete procurement system adequate for both start-up and larger ongoing companies. It includes a discussion of the unique purchasing language and suggested controls and policies.

CHAPTER 9: WORK IN PROCESS

This chapter covers manufactured-part and assembly work order systems that schedule and move parts and material through the manufacturing process.

CHAPTER 10: RECEIVING, STOCKROOM, SHIPPING

Chapter 10 discusses systems for the receiving, shipping, and stockroom functions.

CHAPTER 11: QUALITY CONTROL

This chapter covers the systems required to determine the disposition of discrepant purchased parts and material along with people-oriented concepts for assuring the quality of work in process and finished goods.

7

MATERIAL REQUIREMENTS PLANNING

Material requirements planning (MRP) is the process that determines how many of which items are needed on what date to accommodate manufacturing the product in accordance with the master schedule and the build-ship schedule. The key to successful material requirements planning is to base it on future demand rather than past usage. Predicting future demand based on the past is fraught with problems. For example, if option A has been selling like hot cakes, historical-usage MRP systems will create large amounts of inventory for option A parts and material. Something causes the marketplace to shift demand to option B instead of option A. Result: excess and probably obsolete option A inventory which is no longer needed, and not enough option B inventory to satisfy demand, which will cause backlog to pile up. Unplanned backlog often results in decreased shipments, increased total inventory, and, inevitably, a cash crunch.

Despite the obvious problems with historical-usage MRP systems, many companies use them because data on future demand are not available to the inventory analyst. The inventory analyst is a human computer that orders parts and material by rote formula. Without data on future demand, the analyst has no option except to base future demand on past usage. The usual reason for the inventory analyst being the one to make the key decisions on inventory and work-force levels is that marketing and management, for whatever reasons, simply do not forecast future demand. Marketing people tend to feel that their job is to book orders (which it certainly is), not to get involved with manufacturing's production schedules. In response to the question, "How many units do you think you'll book in September?" many marketing managers will reply, "Ask me October first." Recognize that forecasting future sales volume in specific units is an inexact science. Also recognize that if marketing or management does not forecast future demand, a clerk in the bowels of the inventory department will do it for them.

On the other hand, historical-usage MRP systems are useful in some situations. A typical historical-usage MRP system is called *order-point*.

ORDER POINT

The order-point system for determining requirements is shown graphically in Figure 7-1. Historical usage is combined with lead time to determine an order-point quantity. When withdrawals reduce the on-hand balance to the order-point quantity, a requirement is triggered and an order placed. Theoretically, if usage and lead time remain approximately the same, inventory will be available until the order is received.

The order-point system is useful for inexpensive items with short lead times. Typically, an order-point quantity of parts deemed sufficient to last until a new order can be received is "bagged," with a stock requirement card, Figure 7-2, attached to the bag. When the bag is broken, a requirement quantity and date are noted on the requirement card. The requirement quantity is a judgment call. If data on the card show relatively low usage and quick delivery, a modest requirement quantity is indicated. On the other hand, if usage appears to be increasing or delivery lengthening, a higher quantity is indicated. The card is forwarded to purchasing for ordering. When the order is placed, purchasing notes the purchase order number on the card and returns it to the stockroom. It is placed in the bin with the remaining parts. When the order is received, the received date is noted on the card and an order-point quantity, again a judgment call, is bagged and the card attached to the bag.

In the Figure 7-2 example, a requirement for 100 was triggered on February 12, ordered on purchase order 123, and received on February 20. A

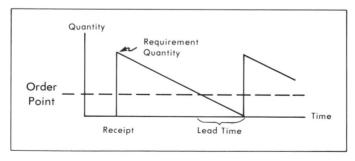

FIGURE 7-1   Order-point material requirements planning system

Stock Requirement			
Part #: ∿		Description: ∿	
Date	Qty	P.O.	Rec'd
2-12	100	123	2-20
4-27	150	456	

FIGURE 7-2   Stock requirement card

requirement for 150 triggered on April 27 has been placed on purchase order 456 and has not yet been received.

There are two basic MRP systems based on future demand: job-lot and forecast-demand.

JOB-LOT

The job-lot system for determining requirements is shown graphically in Figure 7-3. It is recommended in a start-up situation with a single product or a very limited product line. It is also recommended for one-of-a-kind special orders in an ongoing situation. In a start-up situation, management, based on their assessment of future demand, will determine how many units of product to make in a given production lot. The quantity column of each line on the bill of material is extended by the quantity of the lot to determine individual line-item requirements. Production lots are identified by a lot number. The common practice lot-numbering system is the part number followed by a sequentially ascending lot number.

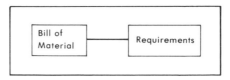

FIGURE 7-3   Job-lot material requirements planning system

The first lot number for model ABC is ABC-001; the second lot number is ABC-002; the third, ABC-003, and so on. Computer-based systems use the part number–lot number system. Because there will probably be more than one production lot in process at the same time, take care to keep material, parts, assemblies, time charges, stock transfers, and stock requisitions segregated by lot. Misapplication of material or parts will create unplanned and disruptive shortages. Mischarged time, transfers, and requisitions will distort cost history.

The job-lot system is also useful in an ongoing business to handle specials—orders that require special modifications to the standard product. In the case of the ongoing business special job, a "special job" bill of material is created. The quantity column for each line item on the special job bill of material is used to determine requirements. Requirements are noted on purchase order forms and on manufactured-part and assembly work orders.

FORECAST DEMAND

The forecast-demand system for determining requirements is shown graphically in Figure 7-4. It consists of combining a future sales forecast with the backlog of booked orders to create a master schedule that accommodates both the backlog and future demand. Each active part number is analyzed and the on-order quantity and schedule adjusted to satisfy the master schedule.

The forecast-demand system is relatively sophisticated in comparison with the job-lot and order-point systems. It is useful in an ongoing situation in which there is a broad product line with many options and a relatively high ratio of common parts. It is often the solution when seemingly insoluble production problems reach a magnitude that seriously impacts the overall business. Among the symptoms are increasing shortages, frequent orders for the same item, "rush" stickers on every work order and purchase requirement, unfavorable labor variance trend, increasing inventory, and shipment falldowns.

To illustrate the forecast-demand system, we will follow the forecast-demand material requirements planning system flowchart, Figure 7-5. The first step is the booking-sales forecast, Figure 7-6. Ideally, the book-

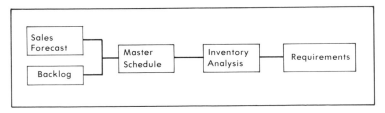

FIGURE 7-14 Forecast-demand material requirements planning system

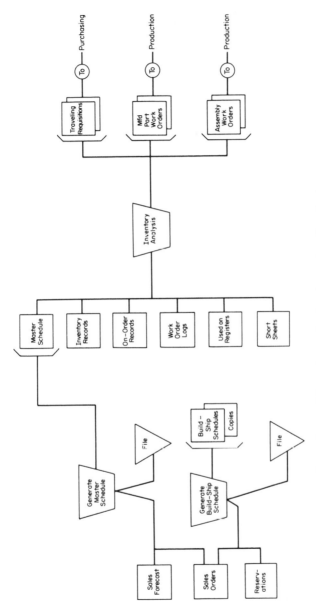

FIGURE 7-5   Forecast-demand material requirements planning system flowchart

Booking-Sales Forecast										Date	_FEB_	
Product/Model	Jan	Feb	Mar	Apr	May	Jun	Jul	Aug	Sep	Oct	Nov	Dec
A	–	10	12	12	8	8	6	4	2	–	–	–
B	28	20	20	22	24	26	26	26	26	28	28	28
C	10	–	2	4	6	8	10	10	10	10	10	10

FIGURE 7-6 Booking-sales forecast

ing-sales forecast should be made on a monthly basis. Bimonthly or quarterly intervals are less than ideal but satisfactory. The forecast should be prepared by the marketing function and should reflect their best estimate of the future booking rate in units. The booking-sales forecast is the vehicle for planning the introduction of new products and the demise of products that are no longer viable. It should be reviewed and approved by management prior to being issued. Management, based on their broader outlook, may modify it. It should be issued a month ahead of the first planning period.

In the Figure 7-6 example, the first planning period is February; the final orders for product A, which is being phased out of the line, are planned for September; orders for ongoing product B will continue through the planning period; the first orders for new product C are planned in March.

The next step is to generate the master schedule and the build-ship schedule. First, generate the master schedule, shown in Figure 7-7. The master schedule should be prepared by or be approved by the manufacturing manager and have the concurrence of top management.

The master schedule is a key planning document. It establishes future levels of inventory and the direct labor work force. It indicates future floor space and capital equipment needs. It is the basis for projecting pro forma cash flow, income statements, and balance sheets. It establishes the planned level of business that governs all facets of the business.

The Figure 7-7 example covers ongoing product B and its options. The first planning period is February. Backlog policy for product B is 30 days minimum and 60 days maximum. To create the product B master schedule, the booking-sales unit forecast for product B is transcribed from the booking-sales forecast, Figure 7-6, to the book-sales forecast line: 20, 20, 22, 24, etc. The February 1 backlog of unshipped product B orders is estimated to be 25, which is entered on the beginning backlog line under planning period 1. Adding the 25-unit backlog to the 20 units forecast to be booked in February gives 45 units available to ship. The 45 units available is entered on the available line under planning period 1.

From this point on, constructing the basic unit portion of the master schedule is cut and try. The name of the game is to keep ending backlog between 30 and 60 days while keeping the build-ship schedule as constant as possible. When sales are forecast at 20 per month, backlog should be between 20 and 40 units; at 22 units per month, between 22 and 44; at 24 units, between 24 and 48, and so on. In the example, keeping the build-ship schedule at 20 per month for the first three planning periods and advancing it to 25 per month in the fourth planning period satisfies the backlog policy and causes only one change in the build-ship schedule.

It is recommended that marketing and manufacturing prepare the options section of the master schedule together. Manufacturing records should provide the recent history of the ratio of various options to basic units. Marketing should know what is happening in the marketplace to

Product _____ B _____				Master Schedule		Date _____ FEB _____				Backlog/Finished Goods Min: 30	Max: 60	
Basic Unit	1	2	3	4	5	6	7	8	9	10	11	12
Beginning Backlog	25	25	25	27	26	27	28	29	30	33	36	39
Book/Sales Forecast	20	20	22	24	26	26	26	26	28	28	28	28
Available	45	45	47	51	52	53	54	55	58	61	64	67
Build/Ship	20	20	20	25	25	25	25	25	25	25	25	25
Ending Backlog	25	25	27	26	27	28	29	30	33	36	39	42

Option	%	1	2	3	4	5	6	7	8	9	10	11	12
1	30	6	6	6	8	8	8	8	8	8	8	8	8
2	40	8	8	8	10	10	10	10	10	10	10	12	12
3	20	4	4	4	5	5	5	5	5	5	5	6	6
4	10	2	2	2	3	3	3	3	3	3	3	3	3

FIGURE 7-7   Master schedule

	Build-Ship Schedule		
B		Date	*FEB*

Ship Date	Sales Order	Quantity	Model
2-10	123	2	B-1
2-10	124	4	B-2
2-10	125	1	B-4
2-20	126	3	B-3
2-20	127	6	B-2
2-20	RES	2	B-1
2-20	RES	2	B-2

FIGURE 7-8   Build-ship schedule

affect options ratios. Based on history and future market feel, option 1 is projected at 30 percent, option 2 at 40 percent, option 3 at 20 percent, and option 4 at 10 percent of basic units. Multiplying these ratios by the build-ship quantities gives the quantities of each option for the 12 planning periods.

The build-ship schedule for product *B* is shown in Figure 7-8. As with the master schedule, manufacturing and marketing should construct the build-ship schedule together. In the example, marketing has elected to reserve two model B-1 and two model B-2 in the latter part of the month for quick turnaround response to orders requiring immediate or very early shipment. If these quick turnaround orders do not materialize, marketing will advance orders for B-1s and B-2s from March to be shipped in February against the reservations. The reservation system is a good tool to provide marketing flexibility by reserving some current month production for quick turnaround orders which would be lost if early shipment could not be made. The build-ship schedule is used by manufacturing to schedule production of the final product, and by marketing to keep customers and sales representatives apprised of ship dates.

The next step is inventory analysis, which is the process that generates requirements for purchased parts and material, manufactured parts, and assemblies. The manual process discussed in the balance of this chapter is the same process used in most computer systems called the *parts explosion*. The parts explosion process starts at the top assembly level for the basic units and options. The process explodes or discloses the quantities and schedule for parts needed at the top assembly level. It then explodes the next lower assembly level, the third level, and so on, then combines the quantities and schedules of common parts from all levels. This final step is the solution to those seemingly insoluble production problems. To illustrate the parts explosion process, we will analyze purchased part number XYZ and assembly B-2. First, part XYZ: management has classified XYZ as an A-value part. The ordering rule for A-value parts is to cover vendor lead time plus 3 months maximum and to schedule receipts on a monthly basis. According to the lead time listing, part XYZ has a 60-day vendor lead time. The vendor for part XYZ will accept orders and ship only in increments of 50 pieces.

A copy of the used-on register is the master listing for inventory analysis. By definition, the used-on register includes each active common and unique part number, noting all its applications and the quantity per application. The working XYZ used-on register, Figure 7-9, has been annotated to note that part XYZ is purchased, is A value, and must be ordered and scheduled in lots of 50 only. It notes four applications for part XYZ. Option 1 for product *B* uses two per, option 2 uses four per, and options 3 and 4 use one per. The inventory analyst will typically lay a piece of scratch paper across the right-hand side of the used-on register

Ⓐ 50 Lots Only Used-On Register			M·A·P P	Sheet *1* of *1*	Description: ∿	Part #: X Y Z
Bill of Material	Description	Qty				
B-1	∿	2				
B-2	∿	4				
B-3	∿	1				
B-4	∿	1				

FIGURE 7-9   XYZ used-on register

FIGURE 7-10   XYZ analysis worksheet

	F	M	A	M	J	J	A	S	O
B-1	12	12	12	16	16	16	16	16	16
B-2	32	32	32	40	40	40	40	40	40
B-3	4	4	4	5	5	5	5	5	5
B-4	2	2	2	3	3	3	3	3	3
Svc	2	2	2	2	2	2	2	2	2
Gross	52	52	52	66	66	66	66	66	66

Short 44
Gross Gross 96
On Hand 0̶
On Hand Assy & Open WO 72

Net   24 52 52 66 66 66 66 66 66
LTSB-3   194 66 66 66 66 66

123 = 50
256 = 100

NET NET
150
44
150
106

NEW REQ = 400

106	90	74	108	92
66	66	66	66	66
40	24	8	42	26
50	50	100	50	
90	74	108	92	

FIGURE 7-11   Short sheet

FEB 10				Short Sheet	Sheet 1 of 1
Part #	Quantity	Work Order	M A P		
XYZ	12	B-2-003	P	PO 123 = 50 w/s 2-10	
XYZ	32	B-1-004	P	PO 256 = 100 w/s 2-20	

and calculate future usage for each application from the master schedule as shown in Figure 7-10.

In the example, service projects two per month usage. The analyst notes the gross requirement per planning period from the XYZ used-on register and the master schedule: option B-2 uses 4 of XYZ per. February gross = 4(8) = 32, March gross = 4(8) = 32, April gross = 4(8) = 32, May gross = 4(10) = 40.

The current short sheet, Figure 7-11, notes a total short of 44 units, 12 on work order B-2-003 and 32 on work order B-1-004. The analyst adds the 44 shorts to planning period 1, giving a gross gross requirement for February of 96 units.

The next step is to check the on-hand balance on the inventory record. The inventory record for part XYZ, Figure 7-12, indicates an on-hand balance of 0.

The next step is to check how many of part number XYZ are in open work orders, using the work order log and the inventory record for all applications of part XYZ. Let's assume that there is a 0 balance on hand of options B-1, B-3, and B-4. The inventory record for option B-2, Figure 7-13, notes an on-hand balance of 4. The work order log, Figure 7-14, for part B-2 indicates two open work orders: lot 003 for 6 and lot 004 for 8.

Inventory Record					Description $\mathcal{N}$				Part # : XYZ
Date	Quantity	Receipt	Withdrawal	On Hand Balance	Date	Quantity	Receipt	Withdrawal	On Hand Balance
1-15	50	✓	—	50					
1-16	38	—	✓	12					
2-2	12	—	B-2-003	0					

FIGURE 7-12   XYZ inventory record

Inventory Record					Description ∿				Part #: B-2
Date	Quantity	Receipt	With-drawal	On Hand Balance	Date	Quantity	Receipt	With-drawal	On Hand Balance
1-20	6	-002	—	6					
1-25	2	—	✓	4					

FIGURE 7-13   B-2 inventory record

Work Order Log				Description: ∿	Part #: B-2
Lot	Quantity	Cut Date	Date Due	Complete Date	
001	6	11-1	12-1	12-10	
002	6	12-1	1-1	1-20	
003	6	1-1	2-1		
004	8	2-1	2-15		
005	6		3-1		

FIGURE 7-14   B-2 work order log

The analyst calculates that 72 of part XYZ are available in on-hand B-2 assemblies and in open work orders for B-2 assemblies: t on hand + 6 in lot 003 + 8 in lot 004 = 18 B-2 assemblies at 4 per assembly = 72. Subtracting the 72 in on-hand assemblies and open work orders from the gross requirement gives a net requirement of 24 in February, 52 in March, 52 in April, 66 in May, and so on.

The next step is to apply lead time setback. Parts B-1, B-2, B-3, and B-4 are subassemblies. Piece parts for subassemblies have a lead time setback of the ship month minus three. This means that subassembly parts should be received in the ship minus three month; the work order will be pulled, staged, and shortages filled in the minus two month; and the subassembly will be assembled in the minus 1 month so that it will be available as a part for final assembly in the ship month.

Lead time setback of 3 months in the analysis worksheet, Figure 7-10, means that the net requirement is moved 3 months to the left, which now makes the February requirement 194 (24 + 52 + 52 + 66 = 194), March 66, April 66, May 66, June 66, and July 66.

The next step is to check the amount on order. The part XYZ on-order record, Figure 7-15, notes a balance due of 50 pieces on order 123 and 100 pieces on order 256.

The analyst calculates that rescheduling both orders to ASAP (as soon as possible) will make 150 units available in February to cover the February requirement of 194. The analyst calculates that 400 units, scheduled 150 in February, 50 in March, 50 in April, 100 in May, and 50 in June, will cover requirements through June. The ordering rules for part XYZ restrict the total quantity covered to a vendor lead time plus 3 months. Vendor lead time for XYZ is 2 months plus 3 months equals 5 months total coverage, or February through June. The analyst notes the resched-

On Order Record							Description: $\sim$	Part #: X Y Z
P.O. # Vendor	P.O. Date	Quantity	Required Delivery	Date Rec'd	Quantity Received	Balance Due		
123 ACME	12-1	100	3-1	1-10	50	50		
256 PEERLESS	1-1	100	4-1			100		

FIGURE 7-15   XYZ on-order record

ule of orders 123 and 256 and the new requirement on the XYZ traveling requisition, Figure 7-16, and forwards it to purchasing.

Let's turn to the part B-2 analysis worksheet, Figure 7-17. The analyst notes the gross requirements from the master schedule: 8, 8, 8, 10, 10, 10. The inventory record for part B-2, Figure 7-13, indicates a balance available of 4, leaving a net requirement of 4 for February, 8 for March, 8 for April, 10 for May, and so on.

Lead time setback for B-2 is ship minus 1. The analyst adjusts net requirements 1 month forward. Lead time setback of ship minus 1 for subassemblies means that they are due to be completed in the ship minus 1 month. To be completed in the ship minus 1 month, they should be scheduled for pull by production in the ship minus 3 month.

The next step is to check the work order log, Figure 7-14, to note what quantities are on order and when they are scheduled for completion. The analyst notes that lot 003 is open for 6 and lot 004 is open for 8. Both are scheduled for completion in February. Therefore, 14 are on order to cover the 12 required in February, leaving 2 to cover the March requirement of 8; this indicates that a new lot, 005, should be cut for 6 units and scheduled for March 1. The analyst notes lot 005 for a quantity of 6 and the due date of March 1 on the work order log and forwards the work order log to the production function.

When the production function has cut the work order for lot 005, they note the cut date and return the work order log to the inventory function.

Traveling Requisition				Description: $\sim$		Part #: X Y Z		
Vendor: ACME			Vendor: PEERLESS		Vendor: ACCURATE		Vendor: PRECISE	
Requisition Date	Quantity	P.O. #	P.O. Date	Vendor	Required Receipt Date			
11-5	100	123	12-1	ACME	3/1 R/S ASAP			
12-20	100	256	1-1	PEERLESS	4/1 R/S ASAP			
X-XX	400				150-2/1 50-3/1 50-4/1 100-5/1 100-6/1			

FIGURE 7-16   XYZ traveling requisition

```
                    F    M    A    M    J    J

        GROSS       8    8    8    10   10   10

      ON HAND       4
                   ___

        NET         4    8    8    10   10   10
                            2
      LTSB-1        12    ⌈ 8   10   10   10
                         ⎪ (6)
    -003=6               ⎪
    -004=8               ⎪ 14
                         ⎪ -12
                         ⎩  2

    -005=6
```

FIGURE 7-17   B-2 analysis worksheet

The result of the forecast-demand material requirements process is a decision on each part analyzed to:

- Leave on order as is. No change from the last cycle is needed.

- Reschedule on-order inward and generate a new requirement.

- Reschedule on-order outward and cancel beyond the A, B, C lead time window.

The essence of the forecast-demand material requirements process, which is ideally a monthly cycle or at most a quarterly cycle, is to accommodate changes in the marketplace which are reflected in the new booking-sales forecast, changes in the actual quantity on hand resulting from random nonplanned withdrawals and receipts, and, finally, to replan part requirements based on the new data. Material requirements planning is a never-ending process, never perfect, but always aiming at theoretical perfection a lead time away.

The XYZ example is about as complex and hairy as they get. Most of them are relatively simple, like the B-2 example. A trained and experienced analyst, depending on the interruption level, should be able to process upwards of 100 part numbers per day through the material requirements planning process. If your part number population is 1000, that is 2 weeks' work for the analyst.

Normally the analyst also does the posting of the inventory record, on-order record, and work order log.

8

PURCHASING

The purchasing function—securing quotations, vendor selection, placing the purchase order, and following up on delivery—appears to be a relatively simple and straightforward process, and it is. In most start-up situations some individual seems to naturally gravitate to performing the purchasing function. As a practical matter, anyone who knows where to procure what is needed can do the job.

This chapter discusses suggested policies for start-up and ongoing companies for the purchasing function and the language peculiar to purchasing, then describes a paperwork system adequate for both the start-up and ongoing situations. First the chapter discusses the purchasing language and policies.

PURCHASING LANGUAGE AND POLICIES

Commitment Log

Because a purchase order issued today is a commitment to pay cash in the future and because cash management is so vital to a new business, it is strongly recommended that a simple commitment log, Figure 16-3, be kept.

The commitment log should be on paper rather than in your mind so that, say, on a Sunday afternoon, you can add up where you are in terms of commitments relative to cash availability in future time periods. Having this data available enables you to plan your cash needs well in advance and avoid running to the bank in a panic to secure additional funds. Bankers do not appreciate panic situations.

The Purchase Order

The purchase order, Figure 16-1, is a contract between you and the vendor binding the vendor to provide and you to pay for X quantity of Y commodity or service at Z price at specified and agreed-to-payment terms and F.O.B. point.

Most requirements are purchased via a purchase order. Formal, typed purchase orders are a luxury that in most instances is not necessary. Most vendors are perfectly happy to enter, process, and ship your order based on a telephone call, or, in other words, a phone or verbal order. Some of them will not even insist on a purchase order number and will enter the order as "verbal from Joe Smith." A written or typed purchase order makes sense and is worth the cost for orders with special terms and conditions.

Purchase Order Number

Purchase order numbers are assigned in ascending sequence for record-keeping purposes. It is suggested that you start with number 1.

Purchase Order Log

A purchase order log, Figure 16-2, is useful to avoid assigning the same number to two or more purchase orders, as a quick reference when you are not sure whether something was ordered or not, and as a cross reference if you file purchase orders in alphabetical order by vendor.

Purchase Order File

Keep all your open or uncompleted purchase orders in an open purchase order file. In a start-up situation, filing open purchase orders by purchase order number seems to make the most sense. When you reach the point where you have several orders open with a single vendor, filing them alphabetically by vendor makes sense. When orders are completed, put them in a closed purchase order file as an audit trail.

Acknowledgment

Large vendors will acknowledge your purchase order with their sales order. Compare these acknowledgments with what you phoned in. If they agree, file the acknowledgment with your purchase order. Resolve discrepancies by a phone call.

Non-Purchase Order Purchases

Most requirements for commodities or services related to the product are purchased via a purchase order. Some commodities and services not involved with the product are better procured using petty cash: postage, minor office supply requirements, coffee for the corporate coffee pot, and similar items. A receipt annotated with what was purchased is all that is needed to account for petty cash expenditures. Airline tickets, personal auto mileage, customer entertainment, hotel accommodations, and similar expenses are usually charged to a credit card and accounted for on personal expense reports. More on petty cash and expense reports is given in Chapter 12, "Accounting."

Requirement

Requirement is the word used to define something that needs to be purchased. Requirements include parts and material for the product, maintenance or office supplies, tools, test equipment, and just about everything else you need to conduct the business.

Requirements for parts and material for the product are generated through the material requirements planning process. Requirements for other items are generated by the person determining the need. Requirements are written up on the purchase order form or a traveling requisition, Figures 16-1 and 16-14. A separate purchase requisition form is not necessary.

Quantity: How Much to Buy

The quantity noted on a requirement reflects the best judgment of the person that generated it and may or may not be the optimum quantity to buy. For example, the material requirements planning process formula may indicate that 137 pieces of something are required. If somethings are priced at $100 per gross or $1 each, 144 is the optimum quantity to buy. Purchasing should be alert to price breaks and should have some leeway to adjust requirement quantities to whatever level makes sense. On the other hand, avoid the temptation to overbuy to take advantage of price breaks. When you are a start-up operation, you cannot afford the luxury of investing heavily in inventory. There is also the ever-present possibility that the product may need to be revised, which could make excess inventory obsolete and worthless.

Approval to Purchase

Make it clear to everyone in your organization from the outset that no one may purchase anything without your specific prior approval. Retaining approval to purchase for you alone is extremely important. Every purchase commitment means a cash payment in the future. Approval is normally of the requirement. In the case where you also want to approve the purchase order before it is being placed, so note on the requirement.

Because of your dedication to the marketplace, you will not always be available to approve a needed or urgent purchase; therefore, an owner absent policy will be necessary so as not to stifle or impede the business during your absence. A few suggestions: for purchase of a major item, allow the order to be placed "subject to confirmation by yourself." If the item is minor, like postage, establish a dollar limitation per transaction. If something is needed for the product (somehow it did not get ordered with everything else), allow a firm order to be placed. As the business grows and your cash situation becomes more secure, approval to purchase can and should be delegated to subordinates. Make sure that your approval delegatees have a clear understanding of their limits to avoid unpleasant surprises.

Vendor

You will be dealing with direct salespeople, distributors, manufacturer's representatives, and independent shops.

A direct salesperson is an employee of the manufacturer. Larger companies tend to use direct salespeople, distributors, or both.

Distributors specialize in a particular type of item, such as electronic components, hardware such as fasteners, sheet metal, bar stock, or plumbing fittings, from a variety of manufacturers. Distributors stock many items and normally can provide quick delivery of out-of-stock items from branches in other cities.

Manufacturer's representatives are usually a small group of salespeople representing several relatively small manufacturers, usually in allied fields. They provide services equivalent to those of direct salespeople.

Independent shops are usually small companies that provide various types of manufacturing capabilities: machine shop, sheet metal, metal finishing, and the like. The owner, like you, is typically his or her own sales force.

Source

A *source* is another term for a vendor. The term *qualifying sources* means to locate and identify several vendors technically capable of providing the same product. The term *source selection* means selecting a vendor from several qualified sources by competitive bidding or negotiation. Ideally, if you have several qualified sources, you can ask for competitive bids and award the order to the lowest bidder with assurance that the product will be satisfactory.

Quotations and Price

A cardinal business rule is that, if at all possible, purchase orders should be on a firm, fixed-price basis. Verbal quotations are every bit as good as written ones. If you have several qualified sources for a given requirement, shopping them will garner you the best price. If a given requirement has only one source, called a *sole source,* good business practice still dictates at least a verbal quotation so that the transaction is on a firm, fixed-price basis.

Recognize that because of time or other factors, you will have to place some orders on an estimated price basis. In this case, select the source based on your best judgment, but follow up to be sure that the estimated price is converted to a firm, fixed price prior to delivery to avoid any unpleasant surprises.

Sales Tax

Most states require vendors to collect sales tax on sales they make to customers within the same state unless the commodity is for resale to another customer. Normally, if you purchase from a vendor in another state you will not be involved with sales tax.

If a commodity or service is used to produce your product or becomes part of your product, it is considered for resale. Your state tax people will issue you a resale number to include in your for-resale statement on the purchase order; this lets your vendor off the hook. Your CPA or public accounting firm can help you obtain the resale number. When you purchase commodities or services that are not destined to become part of your product, such as cleaning supplies, office supplies, and the like, sales tax will be added to the purchase price.

Payment Terms

Payments terms are established by the vendor. How you determine your own payment terms is discussed in Chapter 4, "Marketing." Net-30 means that the vendor expects to be paid within 30 days. $X\%$-10, net-30 means that the vendor authorizes you to deduct $X\%$ if you pay within 10 days. If you elect not to pay within 10 days, the total amount is due in 30 days.

As a practical matter, most vendors do not expect to be paid within 30 days. Most of them will sit still for 45 days, some for 60 days, and a few even longer. In a situation where you have a severe cash crunch, it is possible to formally negotiate significantly extended payment terms with vendors that will enable you to work with their money rather than yours. This tactic, called *dated payables,* is discussed in depth in Chapter 14, "Cash Management."

Special Terms and Conditions

Special terms and conditions are typically:

- Approval of a new tool prior to payment or authorization of a production run
- A situation in which you provide a subcontractor with tooling, materials, or both
- Special shipping procedures, such as those needed to protect commodities that are subject to damage from temperature
- The case in which you must have a certification from your vendor in order to comply with the terms of an order from your customer or to comply with regulatory agency requirements

In the rare cases in which special terms and conditions apply, a written or even typed purchase order is in order.

F.O.B.

F.O.B. translates to "Free on Board," which means where title passes, who pays the shipping cost, and who is stuck with collecting claims for shipping damage. Shipping damage claims are discussed in Chapter 10, "Receiving."

Normally, F.O.B. is the vendor's factory. The reason for this is that it is considered price discrimination to include shipping costs in the commodity price under the theory that if they are included, a customer next door to the vendor's factory is subsidizing shipping costs for another customer across the country. The price discrimination thing is not all that well policed, and it is possible to negotiate F.O.B. your dock rather than F.O.B. the vendor's factory, so give a favorable F.O.B. a shot. F.O.B. your dock also means that the vendor is responsible for collecting shipping damage claims.

Assuming F.O.B. the vendor's factory, there are several ways in which you can pay the shipping cost. The desirable and less paperwork way is to ask the vendor to pay and add. This means that the vendor pays the common carrier when the goods are delivered to the common carrier and adds the shipping cost to your invoice. The reason this is desirable from your standpoint is that you float the shipping charge and only have to issue a single payment to the vendor instead of one payment to the vendor and another to the common carrier. It also is less cumbersome to have the common carrier just drop off the shipment and not have to collect shipping charges when it is delivered or, even worse, to sort out freight bills to the proper shipment.

Delivery Time and Method

Part of the quotation, verbal or written, is when delivery will be made. Normally, vendors will say "from stock if we have it, or a week or two if I have to get it from someplace else, or 30 to 60 days." Unless you have all the time in the world, don't settle for these generalities. Press for a firm date by which delivery will be made, and inform the vendor that you will follow up ahead of that date to ensure it will happen. Do follow up ahead of the promised delivery date. Squeaky wheels get the grease. Additionally, if for some reason the vendor cannot ship when promised, you may have to scurry around and get the commodity somewhere else or, in any event, plan around the delay.

The delivery method, unless agreed to in advance, is normally selected by the vendor and will tend to be the least expensive and the slowest. There is absolutely no way to expedite or trace a parcel post shipment or a shipment via United Parcel Service. It is possible to trace a waybill number from an air carrier, a truck line, or a railroad and expedite delivery. If the delivery method does not matter to you, don't press it. If it does, make it a condition of your order.

Make, Buy, Lease, Rent

Parts, materials, and services (such as metal finish) are either standard catalog items or items unique to your product that are fabricated from your drawings or specifications. It makes good business sense during the start-up phase, while your company is small and struggling, to purchase unique items and services as well as standard catalog items and services. Cranking up and managing an in-house production capability takes management time which, when the business is small, is better spent attending to the marketplace and getting the product to it. When the business is firmly established and the corporate color has turned to green, you can consider in-house production of unique items formerly purchased on the outside.

Certainly in the start-up phase and while the business is small and struggling, you are probably better off leasing or renting capital items rather than purchasing them outright. Suppliers of capital equipment such as test instrumentation or machine tools generally have an in-house leasing arrangement available or will put you in contact with a leasing company if they do not.

A lease is a long-term, generally longer than 1 year, contract whereby the lessor (leasing company) agrees to provide whatever it is the lessee (you) wants at so much per month. A rule of thumb for monthly cost to lease is to divide the price of the equipment by the number of months of the lease to determine the monthly amortization cost. To the monthly amortization cost add the monthly cost of interest at the current rate plus a couple of points on an amount equal to one-half the price of the equipment. Profit for the lessor is a couple of points over their cost of money plus what is known as the residual value of selling the used equipment when the lease is completed. It is possible to negotiate an option to purchase the equipment prior to completion of the lease with a fairly large portion of your lease payments applicable to the purchase price for the equipment.

It is also possible to rent, rather than lease, some smaller items of capital equipment such as typewriters, oscilloscopes, and the like. A rental contract is generally from month to month. A rule of thumb for monthly rental costs is the equipment price divided by 10.

Credit Line

Most vendors are understandably wary of providing commodities or services to new or small, struggling companies without a prior check on your probable ability to pay within a reasonable length of time.

Establishing a credit line is not all that difficult. It starts with your banker. Your bank should be willing to field a reasonable number of credit inquiries relating to your ability to pay. They can indicate the approximate credit line (high five figures or low six figures) and state that their understanding of your corporate policy is to pay promptly. This, coupled with a telephone conversation or a face-to-face discussion between you and the vendor, should establish a beginning credit line which can be expanded and become greater as you develop a prompt payment history.

Select two, three, or four of your most significant vendors and pay them promptly, at least in the beginning. Then, in response to a credit check from another vendor, they will reply that you are purchasing approximately $X per month from them and have paid within, say, 30 or 45 days from their invoice. In other words, assurance from your banker or a prompt payment indication from your other vendors will tend to enable you to readily establish a credit line with new vendors as your cadre of vendors expands.

Sooner or later you will be contacted by credit bureaus with a pitch to provide them with financial and other personal data so that they may include your company in their data bank. It is suggested that you do not respond. Credit bureaus cannot and do not secure a credit line for you. Prospective vendors will still conduct their own checks of references you provide. As you can discover for yourself, credit bureau reports are an excellent source of information about your competition.

Follow-Up and Expediting

The best way to assure on-time delivery or to discover a delivery problem in time to do something about it is to establish an advance follow-up system. An advance follow-up system is quite simple. It consists of a follow-up file of open purchase orders and a disciplined approach to the follow-up process.

In the start-up situation, the follow-up file is the open purchase order file. In an ongoing situation, a good, simple follow-up file consists of copies of open purchase orders filed in chronological order of promised shipping dates.

The disciplined approach to follow-up is to establish a day of the week for follow-up and to do it on that day. It is recommended that all past due orders and orders due within 2 weeks of the follow-up day be expedited by a phone call to each vendor. This system assures two follow-up calls in advance of the promised ship date and one after the promised ship date to ensure that the order was indeed shipped.

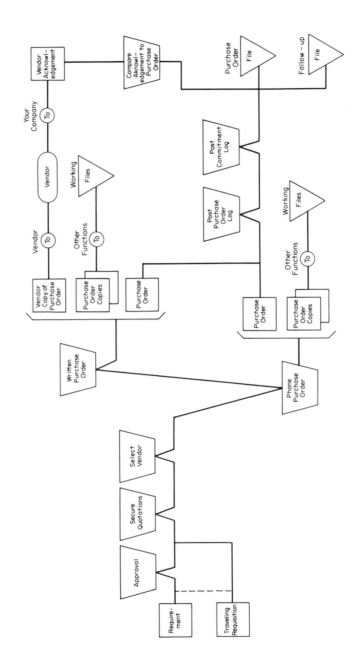

FIGURE 8-1 Purchasing process flowchart

THE PURCHASING PROCESS

The purchasing process flowchart, Figure 8-1, covers the purchasing process.

Requirement

Requirements are generated either on a purchase order form or on a traveling requisition.

Purchase Order Form   The purchase order form, in addition to functioning as the purchase order, also functions as the purchase requisition. The person determining a requirement for purchase notes the quantity, commodity, and required delivery date; signs; and notes the date on the blank purchase order form as shown in Figure 8-2.

Traveling Requisition   When you reach a size that warrants an inventory and production control function or department, the *traveling requisition,* Figure 8-3, makes sense. The traveling requisition is used for repetitive purchases of production parts and material. The person determining the requirement on a traveling requisition, normally the inventory analyst, notes the requisition date, quantity, and required delivery schedule on the traveling requisition and forwards it to the purchasing function. When the requirement is placed, purchasing notes the vendor, purchase order number, date, and promised delivery date and returns the traveling requisition to the inventory analyst.

Approvals

It is recommended that you or your approval delegatees personally approve all purchase requirements generated on the purchase order form. As discussed in Chapter 7, "Material Requirements Planning," the ordering rules or policy you will establish for production parts and materials provide for your personal control or approval of most of the traveling requisitions. Your ordering rules will specify which traveling requisitions require approval.

Purchase Order					

Vendor: *PEERLESS*

JOE   123 - 4567

P.O. # : *123*

Date *1-2-81*

Terms: *NET 30*	F.O.B. *AKRON*	Re-Sale	X	Ship Via:
		Taxable		*UPS*

Item	Quantity	Commodity	Price	Per	Extension
	20	*Widgets*	*1 20*	*Ea.*	*24. 00*
				Total	*24. 00*

If re-sale checked above, all items on this order are for re-sale # *123-456-78*	Requested Delivery: *1-15-80*	Promised Delivery *1-22-80*
Requisitioned by: *SRH* Date: *12-30-79*		
Approved: *SLC* Date *12/31/79*	*YOUR COMPANY*	
Phone ☑ Written ☐	By: *DG*	

FIGURE 8-2   Purchase order

Secure Quotations

If you have several qualified sources and are shopping for the best price, call each of your qualified sources for a quotation on price and delivery. Use the reverse side of the purchase order form for your notes.

If a vendor has already been selected for a requirement, make your place-the-order call sound like you are shopping for a good price, negotiate a bit, and when you place the order, make it sound like that vendor did provide the best deal.

Select Vendor

When all the quotes are in, select the vendor.

Phone Purchase Order

When the vendor has been selected, enter the vendor, purchase order number, date, price, delivery date and method, payment terms, resale or taxable, and other special terms and conditions on the purchase order, as shown in Figure 8-2, and place it by telephone. Copies of purchase orders are not needed until you reach a size that warrants separate material requirements planning and receiving functions.

Written Purchase Order

When a written purchase order is required, it may be Xeroxed, assuming it is legible, or it may be typed and Xeroxed for distribution to the vendor and internally.

Traveling Requisition				Description: 〜		Part #: X Y Z
Vendor: ACME		Vendor: PEERLESS		Vendor: ACCURATE		Vendor: PRECISE
Requisition Date	Quantity	P.O. #	P. O. Date	Vendor	Required Receipt Date	
11-5	100	123	12-1	ACME	3/1 R/S ASAP	
12-20	100	256	1-1	PEERLESS	4/1 R/S ASAP	
X-XX	400				150-2/1 50-3/1 50-4/1 100-5/1 100-6/1	

FIGURE 8-3   Traveling requisition

Post Purchase Order Log

The entry in the purchase order log is made, as shown in Figure 8-4, when the order number is assigned.

Post Commitment Log

Before you file the phone order or written purchase order in the open purchase order file, post the rounded-off total value of the order in the commitment log in the month you anticipate paying for it, as shown in Figure 8-5.

When you have reached a size that warrants having separate purchasing, inventory, and production functions, you probably no longer need the commitment log. Your ordering rules, as discussed in Chapter 7, "Material Requirements Planning," will control inventory purchases to the extent really necessary. On the other hand, if you have become addicted to the commitment log, it can be continued. Bear in mind that it can become an expensive report to keep accurate and current.

Purchase Order File

Purchase orders may be filed numerically by purchase order number or alphabetically by vendor. When purchase orders are complete, transfer them to a closed file as an audit trail.

Purchase Order Log			
P.O. #	Vendor	Date	
123	PEERLESS	1-2	WIDGETS

FIGURE 8-4   Purchase order log

	Commitment Log											
P.O. #	Jan	Feb	Mar	Apr	May	Jun	Jul	Aug	Sep	Oct	Nov	Dec
123		24										
456			128									
789	512											

FIGURE 8-5   Commitment log

Vendor Acknowledgment

Most large, established vendors will respond to either a phone order or a written order with an acknowledgment. Smaller independents may or may not provide a written acknowledgment. If you are comfortable without a written acknowledgment, don't press it. If you want a written acknowledgment, ask for it and follow up to make sure that you receive it.

Compare Acknowledgment with Purchase Order

When you receive the vendor acknowledgment, compare it with your purchase order. Resolve any discrepancies by phone with the vendor and file the acknowledgment with the purchase order.

Follow-Up File

When you have reached a size that warrants separate purchasing and inventory functions, you will have many open purchase orders and should establish a follow-up file. A good, simple follow-up file consists of copies of purchase orders filed in chronological order by promised shipping date. A Monday morning chore for purchasing is to prior-expedite orders due within the next 2 weeks to ensure that they will be shipped or to alert the organization to a shipping falldown.

9

WORK
IN PROCESS

Work in process, called *WIP*, is all the parts, material, and assemblies on the factory floor that the manufacturing work force shapes and assembles into the final product. To the uninitiated, a busy factory appears to be the ultimate in confusion and disorder. In the machine shop, odd-shaped pieces of metal and plastic are milled, turned, formed, or drilled, seemingly at random. In actuality, the machine operators are following exact instructions provided to them in a manufactured-part work order. Manufactured-part work orders contain engineering drawings and production route sheets that inform the operators how many parts they are to fabricate, what size and shape of what material to use, the sequence of operations to follow, what tools and machines to use, and what the final piece part looks like as defined by precise dimensions and tolerances. In assembly departments, assemblers are provided with assembly work orders that define what they are to do. Assembly work orders contain bills of material; engineering drawings; assembly aids such as a model of the assembly, photographs, jigs, and fixtures; and a kit of all the parts to be assembled.

The output of the material requirements planning process for manufactured parts and assemblies is the work order log, indicating that a new lot should be created or "cut," how many are required, and when they should be completed. This chapter describes how manufactured-part and assembly work orders are cut and how they progress through work in process.

MANUFACTURED-PART WORK ORDERS

First, we will discuss the manufactured-part work order system. We will use the manufactured-part work order system flowchart, Figure 9-1, to follow a work order for part PDQ through the manufacturing process.

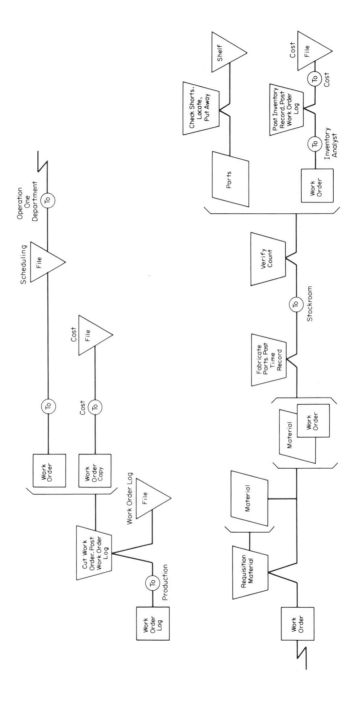

FIGURE 9-1 Manufactured-part work order system flowchart

A requirement for lot 003 covering twenty pieces of part PDQ due on March 1 was determined by the inventory analyst, noted on the PDQ work order log, as shown in Figure 9-2, and forwarded to the production function.

When the production function cuts the work order, they note the cut date on the work order log to indicate that the open work order has been cut and return the work order log to the work order log file.

Cutting or creating the work order is accomplished by applying the work order stamp, lot number, quantity, and due date to a copy of the production route sheet, as shown in Figure 9-3. The time record and stock transfer stamps are applied to the back of the production route sheet. The production route sheet notes the sequence of operations and the departments performing them; this is used to route the work order through the manufacturing process. If you do not have production route sheets, use a drawing. The work order also includes the drawing and other documents included on the bill of material, such as process specifications.

The standard work order numbering system is the part number and a sequentially ascending lot number. In our PDQ example, the work order number is PDQ-003. A separate work order numbering system is not necessary or desirable. Using the part number facilitates identification of work orders on the factory floor. The sequentially ascending lot number facilitates completing open work orders for the same part number in the proper sequence. Computer-based production systems also utilize the part number–lot number system.

Work Order Log					Description: ∿	Part # : PDQ
Lot	Quantity	Cut Date	Date Due	Complete Date		
001	20	12-1	1-1	1-3		
002	20	1-1	2-1	2-10		
003	20		3-1			

FIGURE 9-2   PDQ work order log

Production Route Sheet			Description: ∿	Part #: PDQ
Op:	Description	Department		
1	CUT BLANK	SAW	½" PVC SHEET 6"x 9"	㉒
2	DRILL HOLES	DRILL	PDQ DRILL JIG	⑱
3	SILK SCREEN	PAINT	PDQ SCREEN	⑱
4	STOCK	—	SEPARATE W/PAPER & WRAP IN	
			BUNDLES OF 10 PIECES. ⑱	
			Work Order	
			Lot # 003 / Quantity: 20 / Due: 3-1-80	

FIGURE 9-3   PDQ-003 work order

If you are on a standard cost system, a copy of the work order is forwarded to cost.

The work order is put in a work order scheduling file. Work orders are not necessarily worked in due date sequence. Typical scheduling rules call for parts that are short to be worked first. When all shortages are cleared, work orders should be scheduled in concert with the manufacturing department supervisor. The supervisor can sequence them to reduce setup time. It is recommended that work orders remain in the scheduling file until the day the operation 1 department will actually start to work on them. This practice will ensure that they are worked to the most current need schedule and will keep WIP inventory at an absolute minimum.

When the work order is released to the operation 1 department, the required material is requisitioned from stock and the work order enters the WIP process.

As operations are completed, the operators note their hours on the time record on the back of the work order or on a time record log. The department supervisor notes the quantity completed for each operation on the face of the work order. In our PDQ-003 example, Figure 9-3, 22 blanks were cut. Four blanks were scrapped during the drilling operation, and 18 finished pieces went to stock.

When the stockroom receives the parts, they verify the count and note the actual quantity to stock on the stock transfer stamp on the back of the work order or on a stock transfer log or form. The shortage file is checked, and the parts are located and put away. The completed work order is forwarded to the inventory analyst.

In a rush shortage situation, the stockroom can be bypassed. The total or a partial quantity can be transferred to another work order by the expeditor. In the case of a partial transfer, the balance of the parts are forwarded to stock. In the case of a total transfer, the completed work order is forwarded to the inventory analyst.

The inventory analyst posts the quantity to stock on the inventory record, posts the completion date on the work order log, and forwards the completed work order to cost.

ASSEMBLY WORK ORDERS

To illustrate the assembly work order system, we will use the assembly work order system flowchart, Figure 9-4, to follow lot 003 for assembly B-2 through the assembly process. Work order B-2-003 for 6 units was cut on January 1, as shown in Figure 9-5.

The cut assembly work order consists of a complete bill of material for the assembly with the work order stamp affixed to the face of page 1, as shown in Figure 9-6, and the time record and transfer stamps affixed to the reverse side of the first page. Assembly work orders also include assembly aids such as models, photographs, or sketches.

The cut work order is put in a scheduling file until it is issued to the stockroom for picking. The scheduling file enables the production function to control the order in which work orders get picked. It is recommended that assembly work orders be issued to the stockroom on a daily basis.

In the stockroom, the first step when the work order is received is to note the location of each part on the bill of material. In the Figure 9-6 example, for part B-2, the location for part XYZ is section A, shelf 3, and the location for part 123 is section B, shelf 7.

The next step is to pick the parts and kit them. As the parts are picked, the quantity actually picked is noted on the work order. In our part B-2 example, 24 part XYZ are required for lot 3 (lot 3 has a quantity of 6 and 4 part XYZ are used in each, for a total of 24). Only 12 part XYZ are available, and so they are placed in the kit and the shortage quantity of 12 is circled on the work order. It is suggested that the stockroom circle shortage quantities to facilitate creating the short sheet. Eighteen of part 123 are required; 18 were picked and placed in the B-2 kit.

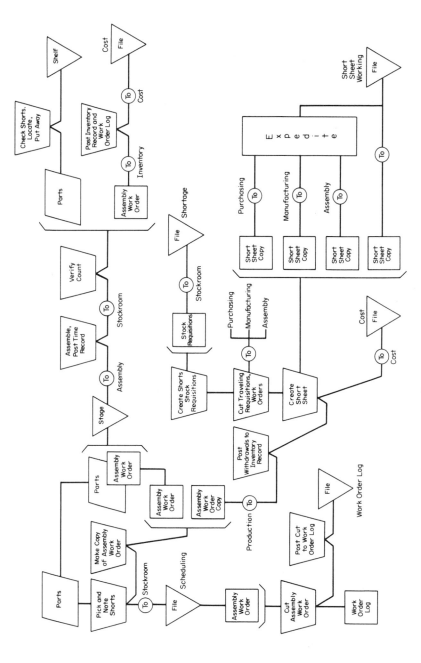

FIGURE 9-4   Assembly work order system flowchart

Work Order Log

					Description: ~	Part #: B-2
Lot	Quantity	Cut Date	Date Due	Complete Date		
001	6	11-1	12-1	12-10		
002	6	12-1	1-1	1-20		
003	6	1-1	2-1			
004	8	2-1	2-15			
005	6		3-1			

FIGURE 9-5   B-2 work order log

		Part #	Description	M A P	Qty		Part #: B-2
1	⑫	XYZ	~	P	4	A-3	
2	18	123	~	M	3	B-7	
3							Bill of Material Sheet 1 of 1 Issued ____ By ____
4							
5							
6							Rev. | Date | E.C.O.
7							
8						Work Order	
9						Lot # 003 | Quantity: 6 | Due: 1-1-80	
10							
11							
12							Description: ~
13							
14							Part #: B-2
15							

FIGURE 9-6   B-2-003 work order

When the pick is complete, the stockroom makes a complete copy of the work order bill of material. The original assembly work order bill of material is placed in the kit with the parts, and the kit is placed in a staging area. The copy of the work order is forwarded to the production function. Production posts the withdrawals to the inventory records.

The production function creates a short sheet and provides copies to manufacturing, assembly, and purchasing. The short sheet, Figure 9-7, notes that 12 of part XYZ are short on work order B-2-003.

The work order copy is then forwarded to the cost function and provides the data on the initial parts and material charged to work order B-2-003.

In preparing the short sheet, the production function notes the part number, quantity short, shortage work order, M-A-P code, and open purchase orders or open work orders. If there is no open purchase order or work order to cover the shortage, the inventory analyst is notified to cut a work order or a traveling requisition. Production also creates a stock requisition for each shortage and forwards it to the stockroom, where it is placed in the shortage file.

Purchasing, manufacturing, and assembly expedite and note the best availability date for the shortages they are responsible for on their copies of the short sheet. Production will meet with purchasing, manufacturing, and assembly and consolidate their data on the working file copy of the production short sheet. If the initial expediting process provides satisfactory availability dates, purchasing, manufacturing, and assembly do what needs doing to make the dates come true. In the event that one or more of the availability dates are unacceptable, the production function bucks the expediting problem to the next level. It is not unusual for a company

FEB 10				Short Sheet	Sheet _1_ of _1_
Part #	Quantity	Work Order	M A P		
X Y Z	12	B-2-003	P	PO 123 = 50 W/s 2-10	
X Y Z	32	B-1-004	P	PO 256 = 100 W/s 2-20	

FIGURE 9-7   Short sheet

president to contact a national sales manager or even the president of a vendor company to expedite an order.

It is recommended that assembly work order kits remain in staging until the assembly department is ready to work on them. The reason for this is that otherwise, people being what they are, common parts will be taken from one kit to fill a shortage in another kit without a transfer transaction, which creates unplanned shortages that will not be discovered until the kit that was robbed is being worked on.

Normally, the assembly work order is completed and sent to stock with the total time expended reflected in individual operator entries on the time record and the quantity completed noted on the transfer stamp on the reverse side of page 1 of the work order. There will be cases in which a partial transfer to the next assembly work order is required. In this case, the partial transfer is noted on the transfer stamp. When the stockroom receives the assemblies, they verify the count and note the actual quantity to stock on the stock transfer stamp on the reverse side of page 1 of the work order. The shortage file is checked, and the assemblies are located and put away. The completed work order is forwarded to the inventory analyst.

The inventory analyst posts the quantity to stock on the inventory record, posts the completion date on the work order log, and forwards the completed work order to cost.

10
RECEIVING, STOCKROOM, SHIPPING

The receiving, stockroom, and shipping functions in small manufacturing companies tend to be performed by a single cadre of people and housed in the same area. All three functions are relatively simple and can be performed by practically anyone. Although the receiving, stockroom, and shipping functions are not complex, they do require discipline and order in carrying them out. All three functions deal heavily in numbers: part numbers, quantities, locations, sales orders, invoices, packing lists, freight bills, and so on. Incorrect count verification in receiving can be costly. Mislocating parts or material in the stockroom can create false shortages and balloon inventory. Shipping the wrong spare part to a customer can cost future sales. Be sure that your receiving, stockroom, and shipping functions are staffed with meticulous people who appreciate the importance of accuracy, order, and discipline. This chapter describes a paperwork system for each function that is adequate for both start-up and ongoing situations.

RECEIVING

To illustrate the receiving function, we will follow the receiving flowchart, Figure 10-1.

When a shipment is received, the first step in the receiving process is to inspect the package for damage. If the package is damaged, describe the damage on a piece of paper and have the person that delivered the shipment sign it, attesting to the damage. The next step is to open the package and determine whether the contents are damaged. If the contents are damaged, set the package aside in the receiving area. If the F.O.B.

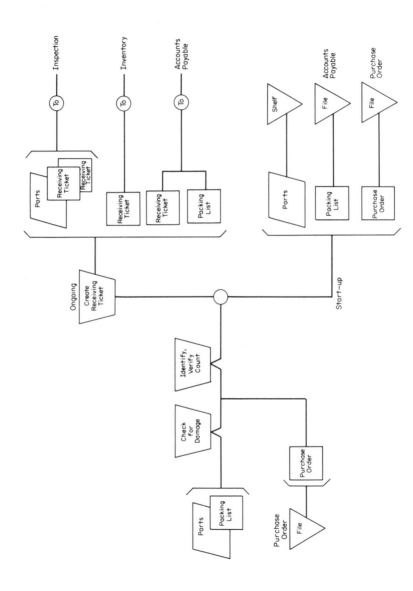

FIGURE 10-1 Receiving flowchart

point is the vendor's dock, you are responsible for collecting shipping damage claims. First, contact the vendor to arrange a replacement shipment. Next, contact the carrier and get your damage claim underway. If the F.O.B. point is your dock, the vendor is responsible for collecting shipping damage claims. In this case, contact the vendor to arrange a replacement shipment and to receive instructions for disposition of the damaged shipment.

If the contents are not damaged, the next step is to compare the packing slip with your purchase order. In a start-up situation, the purchase order is in your open purchase order file. In an ongoing situation with a separate receiving function, receiving will normally have a file of purchase order copies for reference purposes. Make sure that the contents are what was ordered. Count the contents and note your verified count on the packing slip and the purchase order.

In a start-up situation, put the parts in stock and the verified packing list in the accounts payable file to await receipt of the invoice. If the shipment completes the order, move the purchase order from the open to the closed purchase order file. If the shipment is a partial, leave the annotated purchase order in the open purchase order file.

In an ongoing situation, the next step is to create the receiving ticket, Figure 16-34. Forward the original receiving ticket stapled to the packing list to accounts payable. Forward one copy to inventory. Put two copies in the box with the parts and deliver the parts to inspection.

STOCKROOM

A start-up company normally does not need a separate stockroom. Parts and material can be stored on the floor, a table, or shelves. Ultimately, an ongoing business reaches a size that warrants a separate stockroom. Initially the stockroom can be nothing more than a designated area with shelving and racks to store parts and material. A walled-off or caged secure area will be needed when discipline is required to correctly transact parts and material to and from the stockroom.

At some point in time, a locator system will become necessary. In a locator system, rack and shelving units are labeled in some orderly fashion, i.e., rack or shelf unit A, B, C; shelf number 1, 2, 3. The locator system includes a card file with a separate card for each part number currently in the stockroom. The card notes the part number and the location, e.g., 123456 B-2 on the card means that part 123456 is located on shelf 2 of shelving unit B.

An ongoing stockroom also needs a shortage file. The shortage file consists of unfilled stock requisitions, Figure 16-21, filed in numerical order.

To illustrate the stockroom function in an ongoing situation with a separate stockroom, we will use the stockroom flowchart, Figure 10-2.

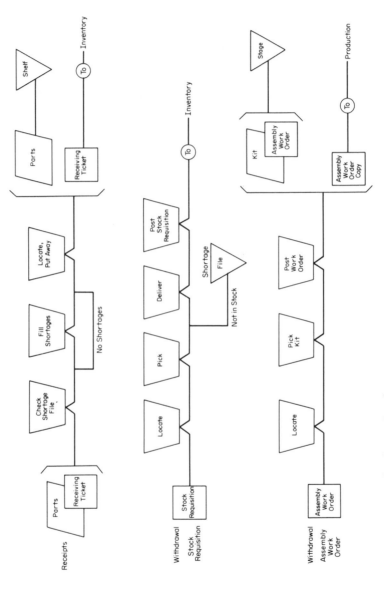

FIGURE 10-2 Stockroom flowchart

Incoming parts will be accompanied by a receiving ticket. The first step is to check the shortage file to see if the parts received are on shortage. If there are no shortages, locate and put away the incoming parts. If there is a shortage in the form of an unfilled stock requisition, fill it. Assuming that there are parts left over, consult the locator file to see if the part has an assigned location. If so, put the parts in the proper location. If the location noted on the card is filled with something else, put the parts in an empty location and note the new location on the locator card. If there is no locator card, find an empty location, put the parts there, create a locator card, and file it in the locator file. Reserving empty shelf or rack space for parts and material that are not physically in stock will increase the floor space allocated to the stockroom beyond what is really needed.

Withdrawals from the stockroom are made by a stock requisition or an assembly work order.

The first step in filling a stock requisition is to use the locator system to locate the part or material. If the requisition quantity is available, pick it and deliver it to the requisitioner, post the stock requisition as filled, and forward it to inventory. If nothing is available, notify the requisitioner and put the stock requisition in the shortage file. If a partial quantity is available, destroy the original stock requisition. Create a stock requisition for the quantity filled, deliver the parts to the requisitioner, and forward the filled requisition to inventory. Create a stock requisition for the shortage quantity and put it in the shortage file.

The first step in filling an assembly work order is to locate each line item on the assembly work order, Figure 10-3, using the locator file. In the example, part number XYZ is in location A-3 and part number 123 is in location B-7. The next step is to pick and kit the work order. This is accomplished by picking the parts and placing them in a box or on a skid. The parts should be bagged or packaged and identified by their part number. In the Figure 10-3 example, the pick is for a quantity of 6 for work order B-2-003. Lot 003 requires 24 of part XYZ, of which 12 were picked and kitted. A shortage of 12, designated by the figure 12 with a circle around it, is noted on the assembly work order. The lot requires 18 of part number 123, and 18 were picked and kitted. The uncircled figure 18 indicates a complete fill. When the pick is complete, make a copy of the complete work order. Place the original work order in the kit and put the kit in a staging area. The copy of the work order is forwarded to production.

SHIPPING

The shipping function packages and packs the product for shipment and processes the shipping documents.

		Part #	Description	M A P	Qty		Part #: B-2		
1	⑫	X Y Z	~	P	4	A-3			
2	18	1 2 3	~	M	3	B-7			
3							Bill of Material		
4							Sheet _1_ of _1_ Issued		
5							By _____		
6							Rev.	Date	E.C.O.
7									
8					Work Order				
9					Lot # 003	Quantity: 6	Due: 1-1-70		
10									
11							Description:		
12							~		
13									
14							Part #: B-2		
15									

FIGURE 10-3   Assembly work order

The shipping assembly bill of material lists all ancillary items that are to be shipped with the product. It also lists packaging and packing material required for domestic shipments. International shipments must be packaged and packed in accordance with specifications provided by your customs broker or freight forwarder.

It is suggested that a shipping kit list noting all ancillary items that are to be shipped with the product be prepared from the shipping assembly bill of material as a shipping aid. It is also suggested that all the ancillary items be assembled on a tabletop and photographed to facilitate proper identification by the individual making the shipment. If packaging and packing is more than just routine, it is also suggested that appropriate steps of the packaging and packing process be photographed as a shipping aid.

When a shipment is to be made, invoicing cuts the invoice and packing list, Figures 16-4 and 16-5, and forwards them to shipping. The F.O.B. line on the invoice and packing list should note whether the shipment is collect, pay and add, or pay and stand. Collect means that the carrier will collect the shipping charge from the customer. Pay and add means that your company pays the shipping charge and adds it to the invoice to be collected from the customer. Pay and stand means that you pay the shipping charges and do not collect from the customer. On receipt of the invoice and packing list, shipping assembles everything to be shipped, then packages and packs the shipment. The packing list is included in the shipment. Shipping notes the shipping charge on the invoice if it is pay and add and either contacts the carrier for pickup or physically transports the shipment to the carrier.

All common carriers have shipping documents called a *bill*—freight bill, air bill, waybill, bill of lading—that they fill out and sign when you turn the shipment over to them. When the carrier has taken possession of the shipment, the actual date it was shipped is noted on the invoice, the shipping bill is attached to the invoice, and the invoice is returned to invoicing. Invoicing then mails the invoice to the customer and distributes all copies.

11
QUALITY CONTROL

The quality control function in a manufacturing company is traditionally divided into three areas: purchased parts and material, work in process, and finished product. In a start-up situation, you make all the quality decisions. Paperwork is not recommended until you reach the size at which it is no longer possible for you to personally make the quality decisions.

The suggested paperwork for work in process quality control is the manufactured-part or assembly work order. It is recommended that you reach an agreement with each employee that a condition of employment with your company is quality workmanship. Once this agreement is reached, simply have your employees sign off on the operations they perform on manufactured-part work orders. If a single individual completes an assembly work order, the completed work order is signed by that individual. If more than one individual worked on an assembly work order, have each of them note what they did and sign it. If workmanship problems are discovered later in the manufacturing process, closed work orders are your audit trail to determine who needs additional training, better tools or equipment, or remotivation.

It is recommended that you control the quality of the final product through a final acceptance test procedure. The final acceptance test procedure takes the form of a list of every characteristic that is to be tested together with the acceptance criteria for each characteristic. Have the individual performing the final acceptance test note the results on the procedure and sign it. The final acceptance test file is your audit trail for corrective action should it be necessary.

At some point on the growth curve it makes sense to initiate a receiving inspection function. Receiving inspection is necessary for no other reason than that it is extremely difficult to return defective product to a vendor several weeks or months after you have received it. Lead time to replace purchased parts or material is also involved. If a defect that makes the part of material unusable is discovered during the manufacturing or assembly process, production will be suspended until a replacement can be obtained.

The balance of this chapter describes a receiving inspection system.

To illustrate a receiving inspection system, we will use the receiving inspection flowchart, Figure 11-1. The box of parts to be inspected and two copies of the receiving ticket are delivered to inspection by receiving. The parts, with one copy of the receiving ticket, are placed in a staging area. The other copy of the receiving ticket is placed in an inspection schedule file. This schedule file enables production to establish priorities for clearing part numbers through inspection in the order in which they are needed. Parts are inspected in priority order as determined by production.

PARTS ACCEPTED

If the parts are accepted, one copy of the receiving ticket together with the parts is forwarded to the stockroom. The other copy of the receiving ticket is destroyed.

PARTS REJECTED

If the parts are rejected, a four-part notice of rejection form, Figure 16-32, is created, noting the part number, description, date, quantity rejected, purchase order number, reason for rejection, and the inspector that rejected the parts.

One copy of the notice of rejection and a copy of the receiving ticket are placed with the parts in a rejected parts staging area. The other copy of the receiving ticket is posted that the parts have been rejected and is forwarded to inventory. It is recommended that the inventory analyst annotate the inventory record and on-order record to indicate the rejection. One copy of the notice of rejection is forwarded to purchasing for their action with the vendor.

Two copies of the notice of rejection are forwarded to production. Production, in conjunction with purchasing, determines whether there are sufficient good parts in stock or in WIP to enable the defective lot to be returned to the vendor for replacement. Return to vendor is the preferred disposition. If the parts are needed for production before a replacement

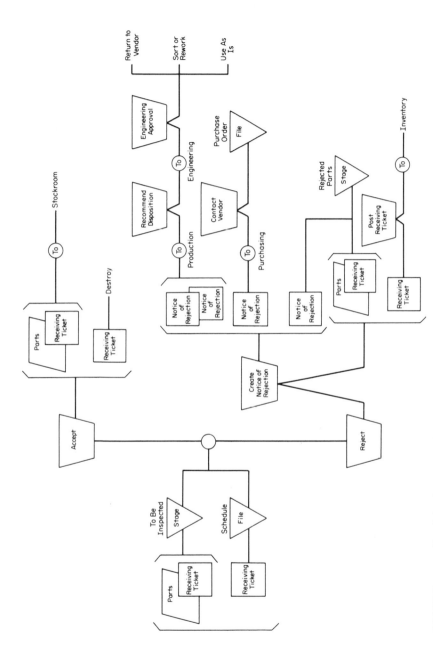

FIGURE 11-1   Receiving inspection flowchart

shipment can be made available, production, in conjunction with engineering, determines disposition and notes it on both copies of the notice of rejection. Engineering should be the final approving authority to accept and utilize sorted, reworked, or defective parts. Disposition will be use as is, sort, rework, or return to vendor if they simply will not function in the product.

To illustrate the disposition of parts to be returned to the vendor, we will follow the return to vendor flowchart, Figure 11-2.

Both copies of the notice of rejection are forwarded to purchasing. Purchasing cuts an invoice and packing list set. The original invoice and a copy of the notice of rejection are forwarded to the vendor. The second copy of the notice of rejection and a copy of the invoice are retained in the purchase order file.

A copy of the invoice is forwarded to accounts payable rather than

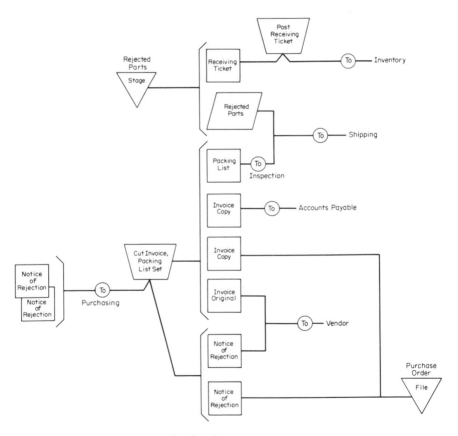

FIGURE 11-2   Return to vendor flowchart

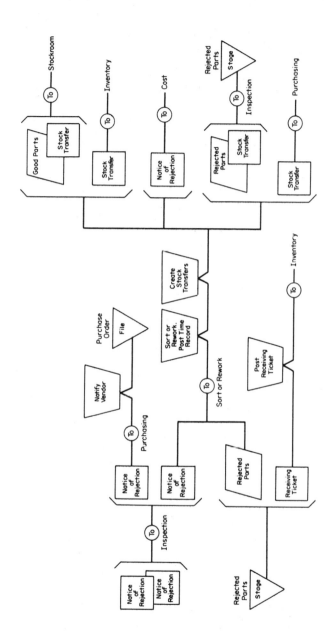

FIGURE 11-3   Sort or rework flowchart

accounts receivable. In this case, the invoice is not a receivable. Your invoice to the vendor is an offset to the vendor's invoice to you and transfers title of the defective parts from you back to the vendor.

The packing list is forwarded to inspection. Inspection forwards the packing list and the rejected parts to shipping for return shipment to the vendor. Inspection then posts the return on the receiving ticket and forwards it to inventory. The inventory analyst should annotate the inventory record and on-order record to reflect the return to vendor.

To illustrate the disposition of parts to be sorted or reworked, we will follow the sort or rework flowchart, Figure 11-3.

Both copies of the notice of rejection are forwarded to inspection. Inspection forwards one copy of the notice of rejection to purchasing. Purchasing should use their copy of the notice of rejection to negotiate with the vendor for the vendor to pay for time consumed in sorting or rework. Most vendors will not reimburse you for sorting or reworking defective material, but some of them will, so give it a shot. Inspection posts the receiving ticket that the parts have gone to sort or rework and forwards it to inventory. The inventory analyst should note on the inventory record and the on-order record that the parts are in sort or rework. The other copy of the notice of rejection and the rejected parts are forwarded to the sort or rework operation.

Operators performing the sorting or rework should record their time on a time record stamp affixed on the back of the notice of rejection. When sorting or rework is complete, the notice of rejection is forwarded to cost to calculate the charge to the vendor.

Production creates two copies of a transfer notice for the quantity of good parts that go to stock and for the quantity of bad parts that are returned to inspection. One copy of the stock transfer accompanies each batch of parts. The copy of the good-parts stock transfer is forwarded to inventory. The inventory analyst should adjust the inventory record and on-order record to reflect the final quantity to stock. The copy of the bad-parts stock transfer is forwarded to purchasing to trigger a return to vendor invoice and packing list set as depicted in Figure 11-2.

In the case of a use as is disposition, both copies of the notice of rejection are forwarded to inspection. Inspection uses the use as is disposition as authority to send the parts to stock, as shown on the parts accepted upper portion of Figure 11-1.

PART FIVE
FINANCIAL CONTROL SYSTEMS

The three chapters in Part 5—"Accounting," "Inventory Cost Systems," and "Cash Management"—provide an overview of the factors involved in the financial control aspects of manufacturing-company management together with specifics on those aspects that directly impact the day-to-day operation of the business.

CHAPTER 12: ACCOUNTING

This chapter describes the general accounting system and its principal components, and provides detailed discussions of accounts payable, terms of sale, invoicing, accounts receivable, and debit and credit memos.

CHAPTER 13: INVENTORY COST SYSTEMS

This chapter describes three inventory cost systems—period cost, semi-standard cost, and full standard cost—and meshes them with the accounts payable and work in process functions. It also describes variance analysis as a management tool.

CHAPTER 14: CASH MANAGEMENT

This chapter explores the difference between cash and profit. It describes how to construct pro forma income statements and cash-flow projections and how to use them to plan and manage cash. It also describes several methods of cash float.

12
ACCOUNTING

The Financial Accounting Standards Board (FASB) is the entity that establishes and maintains the rules that govern the "generally accepted accounting principles" that public accounting firms append to financial statements they prepare for your company. Certified public accountants (CPAs), by definition, must conform to FASB rules. These rules prescribe the format and content of the income statement and the balance sheet, which are the two primary or basic financial statements. FASB has also defined the content of individual accounts: sales, cost of sales, expenses, assets, liabilities, and equity.

An intimate knowledge of accounting principles is not a requisite for successful management of a manufacturing company. Your CPA and banker should provide you with the knowledge and expertise you need to create policy and make intelligent decisions concerning the financial aspects of your business. A working knowledge of accounting systems and an intimate understanding of the portions of the accounting system that impact the day-to-day operation of the business will help you to better manage your company. This chapter describes a typical general accounting system and its principal components, and covers the portions of the accounting system that directly impact day-to-day operations: accounts payable, terms of sale, invoicing, accounts receivable, and debit-credit memos.

GENERAL ACCOUNTING SYSTEM

The principal components of a general accounting system include the income statement, balance sheet, journals, ledgers, source documents, and chart of accounts.

Income Statement

The income statement, sometimes called the profit and loss (P&L) statement, generally follows a set format or sequence.

Sales   *Sales* includes the dollar value of sales of products or services sold to customers. It does not include sales of assets or of anything other than products or services sold to customers. Discounts and allowances, such as trade-ins, are usually deducted from gross sales to arrive at *net sales,* which is the dollar sum of all invoices rendered to customers during an accounting period.

Cost of Sales   *Cost of sales* (COS), sometimes called cost of goods sold (COGS), includes all costs incurred to create the products or services sold during an accounting period. COS includes purchased parts and material, direct labor, and manufacturing overhead or burden that were consumed or incurred to produce the products or services actually sold during the accounting period. Labor, burden, and material (LBM) expended during an accounting period that are *not* part of the products or services sold during the period are *not* included in COS for that period. For example, LBM expended to fabricate piece parts for the stockroom, subassemblies, and finished goods are recorded in inventory asset accounts. When these inventory assets are sold in future accounting periods, inventory is credited (reduced) and COS debited (charged) with the value of the inventory that was sold.

An accurate COS figure for a given accounting period is a hard figure to come by in any business. It is particularly difficult to calculate for a manufacturing company. Chapter 13, "Inventory Cost Systems," is devoted entirely to calculating cost of sales for manufactured products.

Gross Margin   *Gross margin,* sometimes called gross profit, is the difference between net sales and COS: net sales minus COS gives gross margin. A standard cost system enables you to determine gross margin by product and even by option.

Expenses   *Expenses* are costs incurred during an accounting period that are not directly related to producing the product. Expenses may be lumped together but are usually broken out as research and development expense, marketing expense, and general and administrative expense.

Research and Development Expense   *Research and development expense* is abbreviated R&D and is sometimes called product development expense. In a start-up situation it is suggested that all engineering-function expenses be booked under R&D. Because engineering resources are expended on items other than new product development, larger ongoing companies charge only the portion expended on developing new products to R&D. Engineering resources expended in sustaining the existing product line through engineering changes, supporting the factory, and supporting marketing are usually charged to a sustaining engineering account in manufacturing overhead or factory burden. More sophisticated ongoing companies charge marketing support by engineering to marketing expense. An FASB rule requires that all engineering-function expense for new product development be period-costed during the period in which it is incurred. Sustaining engineering can be washed through factory burden, as discussed in Chapter 13.

Marketing Expense   *Marketing expense* includes all expenses incurred by the marketing function except sales commissions paid to independent sales representatives that are not company employees. It includes salaries, travel and entertainment, advertising, sales promotion, preparation and printing of catalogs and price lists, and other such expenses. An FASB rule requires all marketing expense to be period-costed during the period in which it is incurred.

General and Administrative Expense   *General and administrative expense,* abbreviated G&A, includes all expenses not booked under marketing, R&D, or factory burden. An FASB rule requires that all G&A expense be period-costed during the period in which it is incurred.

Income from Operations   *Income from operations* is gross margin less expenses. If no other income is received or expenses incurred, this line on the income statement becomes net before-tax profit.

Other Income and Expense   *Other income and expense* includes items not associated with operation of the business, such as royalty income or interest expense.

Net Before-Tax Profit   *Net before-tax profit,* sometimes called NBT, is the result of adding other income to and deducting other expense from income from operations.

Tax   *Taxes* include federal, state, and local income taxes levied against your company's NBT.

Net After-Tax Profit   *Net after-tax profit,* sometimes called NAT or earnings, is the result of subtracting tax from NBT. NAT or earnings are transferred to the retained earnings line of the equity section of the balance sheet.

Balance Sheet

The balance sheet has three sections: assets, liabilities, and owners' or stockholders' equity. By definition, assets equal liabilities plus equity.

Assets   *Assets* are everything owned by the company or owed to the company by others. *Current assets* are assets expected to be converted to cash within a 12-month period during the normal course of business; they usually include cash, accounts receivable, inventory, and prepaid expenses. *Fixed assets* are assets that are not expected to be converted to cash; they normally include tangible items such as land, buildings, and equipment. *Other assets* are generally intangible items such as patent acquisition costs, goodwill, and the like.

Liabilities   *Liabilities* include everything owed by the company to others. *Current liabilities* include items expected to be paid within 12 months, such as short-term bank loans, accounts payable, and accrued expenses. *Long-term liabilities* include long-term debt, or loans of longer than a year's duration. Liabilities are the portion of the business owned by creditors or others.

Equity   *Equity* includes funds paid to the corporation by stockholders in exchange for stock, and retained earnings. *Retained earnings* are the cumulative NAT earnings, less dividends paid to stockholders or funds drawn by the owners, transferred to the equity section of the balance sheet from the income statement. Equity is the portion of the business owned by the owners or stockholders.

Journals

Journals are called books of original entry. Each financial transaction is recorded as a line item in a journal. For example, each check issued is recorded in the cash journal. Each cash receipt is also recorded in the cash journal. Each journal has a corresponding ledger.

Ledgers

Ledgers are called the final books of record. Each ledger has a corresponding journal. At the end of an accounting period, when the books are closed, all debits and credits in journals are totaled. The journal totals are posted in ledgers. The income statement and balance sheet are prepared from ledgers.

Source Documents

Source documents are those that initiate or record a transaction that is posted on working documents and on books of account. A stock requisition is a source document that is posted to the inventory record and to the appropriate work order and WIP. A time record is a source document that is posted to the appropriate work order and to the payroll account.

Chart of Accounts

A *chart of accounts* is a directory or listing of all asset, liability, equity, sales, cost, and expense accounts in your journals and ledgers. They are usually numbered. You and your CPA will create the chart of accounts for your company. It will consist of accounts selected for your business from a master list of account titles that your certified public accounting firm has in its files. It is desirable that the account numbers be the same as those used in a data processing service available for your use when you reach a size that warrants putting your accounting system on a computer.

Accounting Language

Like any profession, accountants have their own language. The following language interpretations should help you comprehend the three chapters in the financial control system section.

General A complete glossary of accounting terminology would be quite lengthy and is not really necessary to comprehend these chapters. There are many books available for those desiring a broader knowledge of accounting.

Bookings and Sales A *booking* is a receipt of an order from a customer. A *sale* is the shipment of the product and issuance of an invoice to the customer. *Gross sales* are calculated by extending the quantity shipped by the customer list price. *Net sales* are calculated by deducting sales commissions and other allowances from gross sales. For example, assume a gross sale of $100, a sales commission of 20 percent, and a $15 trade-in allowance. Net sales for this transaction would be $65: $100 − $20 − $15 = $65.

Bookkeeping Most inputs to the accounting system stem from the day-to-day operation of the business, usually in the form of source documents. The *bookkeeping* function consists of posting source documents to the appropriate books of account and preparing financial statements. Bookkeeping is accomplished by bookkeepers. Bookkeepers are clerks trained in posting various source documents to the books of account and in preparing financial statements.

Audit Trail *Audit trails* consist of active working documents, closed working document files, and source documents. Audit trails enable auditors from your CPA firm or the IRS to verify that all transactions recorded in your books of account and reflected in your financial statements are correct. For example, audit trails to verify the value of work in process inventory as of the end of the fiscal year are the open work order files in cost accounting. Open work order files should contain stock requisitions for all parts and material charged to work orders and time records for all labor charged to work orders. Adding up all the stock requisitions in open work orders is the audit trail to verify the material content of work in process inventory. Adding up all the labor hours reported on time records in open work orders and extending them by appropriate labor and burden hourly rates is the audit trail to verify the labor and burden content of work in process inventory. Audit trails are also used by operating management in running and controlling the day-to-day operation of the business. If a sales representative makes an urgent request for a demonstrator unit and no demonstrator units are available, the open debit memo file is the audit trail to locate other sales representatives with demonstrator units that might be transferred to fill the urgent request.

Cash   *Cash* is money, usually in the form of a bank account. *Cash in* is money that is received during an accounting period. *Cash out* is money expended during an accounting period. *Net cash* is the difference between cash in and cash out during a given accounting period. Positive net cash, called positive cash, results when cash in exceeds cash out. Negative net cash, called negative cash, occurs when cash out exceeds cash in. Cumulative cash is sometimes called ending cash. Cumulative cash for a given accounting period is calculated by adding cash receipts during the period to cash available at the beginning of the period and deducting cash expenditures during the period.

Cash-Flow Projection   A *cash-flow projection,* sometimes just called cash flow, projects the flow of cash in in the form of cash receipts from various sources and the flow of cash out in the form of expenditures. Cash flow is covered in detail in Chapter 14, "Cash Management."

Pro Forma Statement   A *pro forma* accounting statement is an accounting statement prepared for a future time period based on a set of assumptions.

Assumptions   *Assumptions* are facts or actions that it is presumed or assumed will occur during the period covered by a pro forma accounting statement.

Float   The term *float* means using the funds of others rather than your own cash for an extended period of time. If you charge an airline ticket to a credit card rather than paying cash for it, you are able to float that amount until you pay the credit card company invoice. Most credit card companies allow you to extend the float by paying a nominal monthly finance charge.

The balance of this chapter covers the portion of the general accounting system that directly impacts the day-to-day operation of the business: accounts payable, terms of sale, invoicing, accounts receivable, and debit-credit memos.

ACCOUNTS PAYABLE

Accounts payable includes everything you currently owe to outside vendors, contractors, or others for goods or services rendered. Accounts payable does not include short-term loans or long-term debt. Your CPA will sort out the items that do not belong in accounts payable and will record them in other appropriate liability accounts.

In a start-up situation, accounts payable takes the form of unpaid invoices in a file called "accounts payable." At this point you tend to have only a few unpaid invoices per vendor. Keeping track of them is not a major task. In an ongoing situation, when you have many unpaid invoices per vendor and many vendors, an accounts payable journal makes sense. Your CPA and bookkeeper can set up an accounts payable journal when it is appropriate to do so.

Verified Payables

A vendor invoice by itself is not a payable. To become a payable, the invoice must be verified. Proof that the goods or services were actually received must be attached to the invoice to create a payable. In other words, a payable is an invoice plus a verified count packing list, receiving ticket, or other document proving that the goods or services were actually received.

Parts, material, or other goods delivered to your receiving dock or picked up from vendors are normally accompanied by a packing list. In the unlikely event that there is no packing list, create one, noting the vendor, the commodity, the quantity, your purchase order number, and the date received. In the case of payables for services, the equivalent of a packing list in the form of a piece of paper that attests to the fact that the services invoiced were actually rendered is required. A verified packing list, certified receiving ticket, listing of services rendered, or similar document matched to each paid invoice provides the necessary and required audit trail. Without a verified audit trail, the Internal Revenue Service (IRS) will not allow the paid invoice to be recorded as a legitimate expense.

Vendor Invoice Cost Distribution

It is important that the proper dollar amount of paid invoices be recorded in the correct expense or asset account. This is simply and easily accomplished if an account distribution stamp, Figure 16-40, is affixed to each invoice and annotated by an operating person equipped to assign the proper dollar amount to the correct expense or asset account. If no operating person performs this function, the part-time bookkeeper, who is probably the least qualified person in the company, will make the account distribution decisions. Correct account distribution is important. Maintenance supplies and freight-in charges should not go into an inventory account. Conversely, parts and material purchased for inventory should not go into a maintenance supplies account. Account distribution of paid invoices is part of the total audit trail of the transaction covered by the invoice.

Payment Policy, Dated Payables

Your payment policy sets the time interval between receipt and payment of an invoice. The two prime factors in establishing a payment policy are the vendor and your cash position.

Payment dates for taxes, such as FICA, other withholding taxes, state sales tax, and income tax, are prescribed by law or statute; these taxes simply must be paid when due. Your CPA is aware of these requirements and can establish that portion of your payment policy with you. Utilities—telephone, power, gas, and others—have considerable leverage: either you pay on time or they disconnect the service. If common carriers do not receive prompt payment of freight bills, they will put you on a cash basis. The credit or collection policies of vendors of other goods and services vary widely. Through experience or experimentation you can determine which vendors enforce their payment terms, which are flexible, and how flexible they are. Vendors that have a net 30-day policy rarely expect to be paid within 30 days from the date of their invoice. Most will sit still for 45 days, some for 60 days, and others even longer.

Your cash position is a key factor in the execution of your payment policy. If $10,000 worth of unpaid invoices is due for payment on the first of the month and your bank balance is $7000, $3000 worth of invoices will not be paid on the first of the month. In this case you rank-order invoices, with the starchy vendors such as the IRS, utilities, and common carriers on top, followed by vendors of goods and services in the order of their relative flexibility.

Let's discuss the discount incentive for prompt payment. Some vendors offer a discount of a percentage of the total invoice price if the invoice is paid within a relatively short time. Typical such policies are 1%-10 days or 2%-10 days, net due in 30 days. Let's assume that you have $10,000 worth of invoices with payment terms of 2%-10, net 30. If you pay within 10 days, you save $200. Let's further assume that you must borrow the $9800 at 20 percent annual interest in order to pay within 10 days. Twenty percent annual interest on $9800 for 20 days is $107.40, or $92.60 less than the $200 you will save by paying within 10 days. If your cash position will allow it, you should seriously consider a payment policy that takes advantage of discounts for prompt payment.

Let's move on to the payment policy itself. In a start-up situation your payment policy is usually you sitting down with your file folder of unpaid invoices over a weekend when things are quiet, paying those you decide to pay, and leaving those you decide not to pay in the folder of unpaid invoices. Having the purchase commitment report at hand will help you decide which ones to pay now and which ones to defer. In an ongoing situation, you will ultimately reach a point at which it is no longer practical for you to personally sort through unpaid invoices and decide which to pay and which to defer. At this point a payment policy becomes necessary so that someone else can sort through the unpaid invoice file and use the same decision process you use in deciding which ones to pay and which ones to defer. Your policy is a list of decision rules for rank-ordering payables and determining which payables are to be floated for how long. If your cash position is such that you are not secure in letting your invoice payer proceed independently, arrange for a schedule of invoices due for payment to be provided to you a week in advance so that you can either decide to defer some or arrange to have sufficient cash available to cover the checks that will be issued on the payment date.

Aged Payables

If you pledge receivables for short-term loans between issuing an invoice and receiving payment, your banker will probably insist on an aged payables report on a monthly basis. Even if you do not need an aged payables report for your banker and you have reached the point where someone else is paying invoices, an aged payables report is helpful in planning short-term cash. An aged payables report is relatively simple to prepare. It is a six-column report with the following column headings: Vendor, 0–30, 30–60, 60–90, 90+, Total. There is a line for each vendor. The dollar amounts owed each vendor are aged and totaled in the appropriate column. Recently received invoices, those not more than 30 days old, are totaled in the 0–30 column. Those that are more than 60 and less than 90 days old are totaled in the 60–90 column. The total owed to each vendor is listed in the total column. Each of the columns is totaled.

Petty Cash

Petty cash is a nomimal amount of cash kept on hand to pay for minor purchases that do not warrant a purchase order. When it is initially set up, a check is issued "to establish a petty cash fund." As petty cash is used, it will need to be replenished. When it reaches the replenishment point, add up the total of all receipts covering disbursements of petty cash and issue a check "to replenish petty cash" in the amount of the cash disbursed. Bundle all the receipts together, note the check number and the date of the check, and file the bundle in a petty cash file as an audit trail.

Expense Reports

When you are in a start-up situation, it is recommended that you and anyone else who will be involved in travel or entertainment of customers arm yourselves with several credit cards. Avoid cash advances. Use credit cards whenever possible. The reason for this is that a credit card account gives you at least 30 days' worth of float. Most of them allow a significantly longer float with a monthly finance charge, which will be very close to what you pay the bank for money. The reason for recommending against cash advances is that it allows the person receiving the advance to float your company. If a cash advance is necessary, insist on an expense report the day after the traveler returns home, or at the outside within a week of the return date. Business travelers tend to procrastinate in filling out and submitting expense reports. Cash advances to frequent travelers who procrastinate can reach sizable amounts. Expense reports can be nothing more than a piece of paper noting the traveler's name, the date of the trip, the purpose of the trip, and an itemization of expenses. The IRS requires receipts for practically everything, so make it clear that all hotel or motel expenses, meals, transportation, and everything else possible be documented by receipts attached to the expense reports.

TERMS OF SALE

Terms of sale normally include two factors: *F.O.B. point* and *payment terms.* Historical imperatives in your industry may dictate your terms of sale. If all your competitors absorb shipping costs and offer a prompt payment discount, you may have to offer the same terms to remain competitive. On the other hand, terms of sale are cost factors. Once you have established your terms of sale, it is easy to make them more liberal and very difficult to make them more conservative. Take some time to think through what you can afford and what terms of sale make the most sense for your particular situation.

F.O.B. Point

Unless there is some compelling reason to offer F.O.B. your customer's dock, it is recommended that your F.O.B. point be your dock. F.O.B. your dock means that title transfers from you to your customer when the carrier takes possession of the shipment. This in turn makes your customer responsible for collecting shipping damage claims. F.O.B. your dock also means that the customer pays the shipping charges. There are two methods of handling shipping charges: collect, and pay and add. If you ship collect, the common carrier will arrange to either invoice the customer after delivery or collect from the customer when delivery is made. Pay and add means that you pay the common carrier and add the shipping charges to your customer invoice.

F.O.B. your customer's dock means that you pay shipping charges. Title transfers when the shipment arrives at your customer's dock, which makes you responsible for collecting shipping damage claims.

Payment Terms

Payment terms are discounts for prompt payment and the time interval between the invoice date and when you ask for payment. The converse of the prompt payment discount example previously discussed applies if you elect to offer prompt payment discounts to your customers. In other words, you can save money by taking advantage of prompt payment discounts offered by your vendors, and it will cost you if you offer a prompt payment discount and your customers take advantage of it.

The payment period, or the time interval between the invoice date and when you request full payment, is a variable. The maximum is normally 30 days. The minimum can be zero days. You can specify net due on shipment or net due on delivery. One company the author has worked with has a product that requires installation by a service professional. They have a net on installation payment policy. Their product is manufactured by a complete subcontractor that invoices them when the product is shipped and whose payment terms are net 30 days. They discuss their net on installation payment terms with the customer prior to booking the order and again prior to shipment, and press the customer to have a check ready for their service representative when the installation is completed. They are not 100 percent successful in enforcing this policy, but in the majority of cases they collect from the customer before they have to pay their complete subcontractor, which is the best of all cash-flow worlds.

INVOICING

It is recommended that you forward your invoice to the customer on the same day that shipment is made. The *invoice* is the document that creates a receivable and the document that triggers the collection process. The collection process provides cash, which is the lifeblood of the enterprise.

Invoice–Packing List Set

The invoice–packing list set normally consists of:

- Invoice original   To customer
- Invoice copy   To customer
- Invoice copy   To sales representative
- Invoice copy   To service representative
- Invoice copy   To sales order file
- Invoice copy   To accounts receivable file
- Packing list   With shipment

As shown in Figures 16-4 and 16-5, the format of the invoice and packing list is the same, except that the pricing data are blanked out on the packing list.

Invoice Log

The invoice log, Figure 16-6, is a combination audit trail and mechanism to avoid assigning the same invoice number to two or more invoices. The simplest and most straightforward invoice numbering system starts with number 1 and proceeds in ascending number sequence.

ACCOUNTS RECEIVABLE

A customer invoice becomes a *receivable* when it is mailed or otherwise delivered to the customer. Your customer's system for processing invoices for payment will probably be similar to yours. Invoices received in the mail will go into a suspense file, awaiting receipt of the shipment and a verified packing list or receiving ticket. When a verified packing list or receiving ticket has been matched and attached to an invoice, the invoice and packing list are placed in an accounts payable suspense file to await payment in accordance with your customer's payment policy or, depending on your customer and other factors, it could enter an approval process. Some customers, particularly large companies, large institutions, and government agencies, have some form of approval process that an invoice must go through prior to payment. Ultimately, when all approvals and other factors have been taken care of, your invoice will be inserted in a queue for payment. Your customer, like yourself, may overtly delay payment in order to enhance cash flow.

Advance Arrangement for Prompt Payment

Some people are extremely reluctant or have an inhibitive hang-up about asking customers for payment either before or after invoicing. As a struggling entrepreneur, you cannot afford the luxury of such a hang-up. It is perfectly legitimate to discuss payment with your customer prior to making shipment. Feel free to ask if there is an approval process and, if so, what factors are involved in the approval process and what you can do to accelerate it. Point out that you are a small business with limited cash resources; unlike Fortune 500 companies, you must receive prompt payment in this era of tight money supply, and so on. Surprisingly, most large companies, institutions, and government agencies will bend over backward to assist small businesses, particularly when you make your case in advance. As previously noted, it is even possible to arrange for a check to be available when your product is delivered. Recognize that you will not always be successful in your attempts to arrange prompt payment in advance; however, you have nothing to lose by trying it. More often than not, you will be successful.

Accounts Receivable Follow-Up File and System

The accounts receivable follow-up file is simply a file of all unpaid invoices. As payments are received, they are posted on the accounts receivable file copy of the invoice. If the payment is a partial payment, the invoice remains in the open file. If the payment is complete, the invoice is annotated and retained in a paid invoice file as an audit trail.

The accounts receivable follow-up system consists of everything you can possibly think of to accelerate payment of your invoice. Do whatever needs doing to keep your customer's excuse file for nonpayment of your invoice completely empty. The way to do this is to either physically or by telephone walk through the entire customer payment process and make sure that all the t's are crossed and the i's dotted, so that the only remaining excuse for nonpayment is "our policy is not to pay until x days have elapsed." When you reach this point, commence ascending the pecking order of authority in the customer's organization until you find the person who can direct that payment be made. Then go back and start the walk-through again to ensure that the underlings have followed instructions. The collection process is hard, unpleasant, and often frustrating work. The recommended approach stresses personal contact at the customer's facility or by telephone rather than correspondence. Dunning letters are easily filed away. Repetitive personal contacts are like squeaky wheels . . . they get the grease.

Aged Receivables

As with aged payables, discussed previously, your banker will want monthly aged receivables reports if you pledge receivables for short-term loans covering the time period between issuing the invoice and collecting it. The format is the same as the aged payables report. Even if you do not need an aged receivables report for your banker, it is still recommended as a tool to highlight your problem accounts and trigger action on your part and that of your sales and service representatives.

DEBIT-CREDIT MEMOS

A *debit memo,* Figure 16-26, is similar to an invoice. An invoice is normally issued when product is shipped to a customer against a customer purchase order. The customer is expected to pay the invoice. A debit memo is used when it is necessary to record the fact that you have a dollar claim against a second party, but the second party is not expected to pay it.

A *credit memo* is similar to an invoice to you from a second party; it is used to record the fact that the second party has a dollar claim against your company that is not expected to be paid.

Debit and credit memos are infrequently used and are not really necessary in a start-up situation. In a start-up situation you can use a regular invoice labeled "memo invoice" in lieu of a debit memo. You can also use a regular invoice labeled "credit memorandum" in lieu of a credit memo. Debit-credit memo forms tend to be used when you add a professional accountant to your staff. Debit-credit memos, like memo invoices or credit memorandum invoices, are nothing more than an audit trail to record a dollar claim against a second party or from a second party against your company which will be resolved by some method other than payment.

Use of Debit-Credit Memos

When you subcontract fabrication of a piece part and provide the tooling to the subcontractor, a debit memo is used to record on your books and the subcontractor's books that you have furnished the tooling and expect it returned when the job is complete. When the job is complete and the tooling is returned, a credit memo is issued to offset the debit memo, and the transaction is completed.

When you provide a demonstrator unit to a customer or a sales representative, a debit memo is used to record the fact. When the demonstrator unit is returned, a credit memo is issued to offset the debit memo. A customer invoice issued to cover the sale of a demonstrator unit also offsets a debit memo.

Debit and credit memos are used in any case in which it is necessary to provide a memorandum of a dollar liability from a second party to your company or from your company to a second party where the transaction will be completed without payment being made either way.

13
INVENTORY
COST
SYSTEMS

As discussed in Chapter 12, "Accounting," determining an accurate or even an approximate cost-of-sales figure for a manufacturing company can be difficult. Accounting theory says add all expenditures for labor, burden, and material during an accounting period to the inventory value at the beginning of the period and deduct the inventory value at the end of the period to derive cost of sales for that period. Taking a physical inventory every month will, in fact, produce an accurate cost-of-sales figure. However, a monthly physical inventory is not always practical and, in most cases, is not economically feasible for a manufacturing company. Additionally, the monthly inventory approach does not provide variance data, which, as discussed later in this chapter, is an extremely valuable management tool to gauge factory performance.

Many companies establish what they believe to be an accurate cost-of-sales ratio (cost of sales divided by sales) and extend monthly sales by that ratio to derive monthly cost of sales. On the surface, the ratio approach seems valid, but it is fraught with potential errors. The cost of purchased parts and material changes as the months roll by—usually in an upward direction. Labor cost per unit of product also varies from production lot to lot—again usually in an upward direction. If costs creep up from month to month and the ratio is not changed to reflect the upward creep, profit and inventory will be overstated, and this can result in a sizable adjustment at the close of the fiscal year when a physical inventory is taken. One company the author has worked with used the same ratio for several years and did not take year-end physical inventories. When this company required certified financial statements, their CPA insisted on a physical inventory. Their inventory was so far overstated that the downward adjustment all but wiped out retained earnings. What had appeared to be a profitable operation turned out to be a little better than break even.

The solution to the manufacturing-company cost-of-sales dilemma is an inventory cost system. This chapter covers three different inventory cost systems: period cost, full standard cost, and semistandard cost.

Period Cost System

The term *period cost* means cost or expense incurred during an accounting period. An accounting period is usually a calendar month, a quarter, or a year. In the context of inventory cost systems, a period cost system means that you record all inventory purchases and all labor used to create inventory in a given accounting period as a cost or expense incurred in that period. In other words, you period-cost all inventory purchases and all labor expense in the month they are incurred. There is no inventory asset on the balance sheet.

A period cost system records the maximum possible amount of deductible costs or expenses for inventory purchases and paid direct labor in a taxable year.

Full Standard Cost System

In a *full standard cost* system, a standard cost in dollars is determined and established for each purchased part and unit of measure for each type of purchased material. Standard hours and standard material dollars are determined and established for each manufactured part and assembly. Standard direct labor rates and standard burden rates are also established. *Burden,* also called *overhead,* is indirect factory expense.

Under a full standard cost system, all parts, material, labor, and burden are transacted into inventory and stay in inventory until the end product is sold. When the product is sold, inventory is credited or reduced by the standard cost, and cost of goods sold is debited. Inventory is recorded as an asset on the balance sheet.

Semistandard Cost System

A semistandard cost system is appropriate in a situation in which, for whatever reason, an inventory asset is desired on the balance sheet and a full standard cost system is not needed or appropriate. As the term "semi" implies, a semistandard cost system falls roughly halfway between a period cost system and a full standard cost system in complexity and usefulness as a management tool.

Period Cost vs. Standard Cost

There are pros and cons to each system. A period cost system is very simple. In fact, it is really not a system at all. Paying vendor invoices and employees is all that a period cost inventory system entails.

A full standard cost system, on the other hand, is relatively complicated or sophisticated. A full standard cost system requires establishing standards in the first place and a transaction each time a part, material, or labor is charged to a work order. In return for all the effort required to establish and operate it, a full standard cost system provides one of the best tools available to enhance the productivity of a manufacturing operation: variance reports.

A full standard cost system will enhance profit in the first years. A period cost system will record the maximum possible deductible expenses, which will reduce profit in the first years. A simple example illustrates the effect of a period cost or full standard cost inventory cost system on the income statement and balance sheet. Assume that XYZ corporation manufactured 100 widgets at $10 per widget and sold 50 widgets at $20 per widget in a given accounting period.

Under a period cost inventory cost system, the income statement would look like Figure 13-1. The balance sheet would have zero inventory recorded as an asset.

Under a standard cost system, the income statement would look like Figure 13-2. Inventory of $500 would be recorded as an asset on the balance sheet.

When you start a new business, you may elect to start with a period cost, a full standard cost, or a semistandard cost inventory cost system. If you elect to start with a standard cost system, you will probably stay with standard cost forevermore. If you elect to start with a period cost system,

Sales:	50 units	$20	$1,000
Expenses:	100	$10	$1,000
Income			-0-

FIGURE 13-1   Period cost income statement

Sales:	50 units	$20	$1,000
Cost of Sales:	50	$10	$ 500
Income			$ 500

FIGURE 13-2   Standard cost income statement

you can stay with it until you convert to a standard cost system of your own volition or until the first IRS audit of your tax return. Assuming that your tax returns are prepared by a CPA, the IRS will normally wait several years before conducting their first audit. Chances are they will insist that you convert from period cost to standard cost when their first audit is completed. Standard cost systems are considered accepted accounting practice for ongoing manufacturing businesses.

Simplicity or complexity considerations aside, if your objective is to doll up your new business from the outset to make it attractive to a prospective acquiror, the standard cost approach may appear to be the way to go. You will record the maximum possible profit and will have a good tangible inventory asset on the books as well. In a start-up situation, the first year normally produces minute, if any, profit, and so cash drain to pay taxes is usually not a major factor in the decision between a period cost or a standard cost inventory cost system.

On the other hand, the standard cost approach will consume considerable entrepreneur time and cash to pay the cost accountant. Unless there are compelling reasons for a standard cost system, a start-up business is much better off with a period cost system. If you do start with a period cost system and later convert to a standard cost system, you will record a whopping profit in the year you convert. The reason for this is that while you were under a period cost system, all material, parts, and labor were expensed against profit and nothing was recorded on the balance sheet as an asset. When you convert, the total value of your on-hand inventory is recorded on the balance sheet as an asset. The offsetting accounting entry is a credit to expense and a debit to profit equal to the inventory value.

PERIOD COST INVENTORY COST SYSTEM

There are two types of period cost systems: cash and accrual.

The cash approach is the simplest and most straightforward. You record inventory expense in the month in which the expense is paid. In other words, if you purchase and are invoiced for something in January but do not pay for it until March, you record the expense in March.

The accrual system means that you record the cost or expense in the period in which you incur it, not in the period in which you pay for it. In other words, if you purchase and are invoiced for an inventory item in January but do not pay for it until March, you record it as an expense or cost in January and accrue the cost or expense in accounts payable. The accrual system provides the maximum deductible cost or expense in a taxable year.

The only real difference between a cash system and an accrual system is the month or accounting period in which you record the inventory cost or expense: under a cash system, inventory cost or expense is recorded in the month paid, whereas, under an accrual system, an inventory cost or expense is recorded in the month the vendor invoice is received. In either system labor is period-costed the month you pay your employees. The period cost inventory cost system flowchart in Figure 13-3 illustrates the cash and accrual approaches.

A period cost system does not provide an actual or accurate monthly cost-of-sales figure. Monthly profit will vary depending on the volume of inventory purchases and sales volume. If monthly sales volume is constant, profit will vary inversely with the magnitude of inventory purchases. A large-inventory-purchases month will be a low-profit month. A low-inventory-purchases month will be a high-profit month. If monthly purchases are constant, profit will vary directly with sales volume. A high-sales month will be a high-profit month. A low-sales month will be a low-profit month. Monthly profit fluctuations tend to average out over a year's time. Profit recorded under a period cost system, even though it fluctuates from month to month, is an accurate and honest figure. Period cost systems completely avoid any year-end adjustments to profit.

FULL STANDARD COST INVENTORY COST SYSTEM

Under a full standard cost system, standard costs are established for all products released for repetitive and ongoing production. Standard costs are used to value inventory purchased from vendors, manufactured, and assembled in-house. There are three classifications of inventory.

Stockroom Inventory: Stockroom inventory is inventory that has been transacted into the stockroom either as a receipt from a vendor or as a stock transfer from a completed manufactured-part or assembly work order.

Work in Process: Work in process inventory (WIP) is inventory that has been transferred from the stockroom to an open manufactured-part or assembly work order.

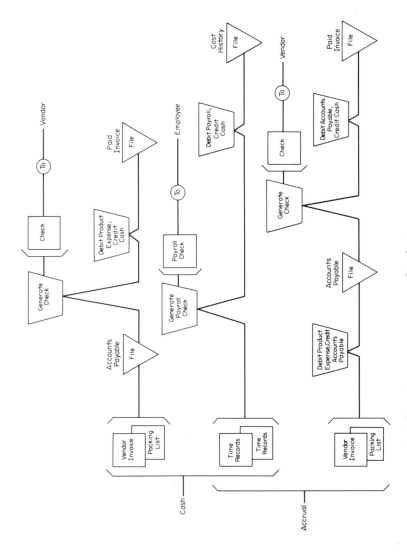

FIGURE 13-3   Period cost inventory cost system flowchart

166

Finished Goods Inventory: Finished goods inventory includes inventory transferred from completed manufactured-part or assembly work orders.

A copy of each inventory transaction is provided to the cost accounting (cost) function. Cost uses the transactions to:

- Transact parts and material from one inventory classification to another at standard cost
- Calculate actual cost and variance from standard cost
- Value each classification of inventory
- Calculate an accurate cost-of-sales figure for product sold during a given accounting period
- Provide an audit trail to enable your CPA or public accounting firm to audit inventory transactions so that they can and will certify the balance sheet and income statement

The work order is the bucket that collects all parts, material, and labor used to manufacture parts and assemblies as well as being the vehicle that moves inventory through the manufacturing process. The work order system is illustrated in Figure 13-4.

To illustrate the standard cost inventory cost system, we will discuss how standard costs are determined and revised, the use of the cost history record, how work order transaction source documents serve as the basis for material and labor charges to work orders and WIP, how the cost function uses these transaction source documents to accumulate material and labor charges against work orders, and how these charges are distributed back to inventory. We will also discuss the variance report, which is a key management tool for monitoring and improving factory operations.

STANDARD COST, GENERAL

Standard costs for purchased parts and material, manufactured parts, and assemblies are determined differently. Once standard costs are established, they normally remain in effect for 1 year or longer. In an era of double-digit inflation, it makes sense to revise standard costs annually. When inflation is moderate, it makes sense to revise standard costs less often than at annual 12-month intervals. When standards are revised, it is recommended that variance reports for at least the prior 1-year period

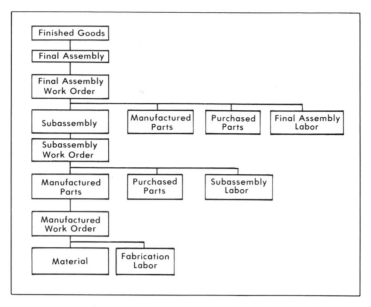

FIGURE 13-4   Work order system

be adjusted to the new level to preserve variance trend analysis on the same baseline.

Purchased Parts and Material Standard Costs

In the process of purchasing the initial sets of parts and material for engineering or prototype models, it is customary to secure price quotations for purchased parts and material in the quantities anticipated for production. It is recommended that the initial purchased parts and material standard costs be established at anticipated production quantity prices.

As purchased parts and material invoices are paid, the actual price per part or unit of measure is posted on cost history records. Cost history records are used to revise standard costs.

Manufactured-Part Standard Costs

The standard cost for a manufactured part comprises material and labor. The material standard cost is the gross unit of measure quantity required to make the part extended by the purchased material standard cost per unit of measure. If a blank of 6″ × 9″ is required to manufacture a part measuring 5″ × 8″, the gross unit of measure is 6″ × 9″.

The labor standard is expressed as both standard direct labor hours per part and standard hourly labor and burden dollars per part. There are as many theories on how to establish standard labor hours for manufactured parts as there are graduate industrial engineers. It is recommended that a knowledgeable person make a judgment call in establishing the gross unit of measure standard quantity and standard labor hours per part, with or without creating a production route sheet.

Actual material costs and labor hours and dollars are posted to cost history records when manufactured-part work orders close. Cost history records are used to revise standard costs.

Assembly Standard Costs

Assembly standard costs have four components: purchased parts and material used in the assembly, manufactured parts used in the assembly, lower-level subassemblies used in the assembly, and labor hours to assemble.

It is recommended that cost use a working copy of the bill of material to establish and record standard cost for assemblies. This record is the back-up or audit trail for assembly standard costs recorded on assembly cost history records. Cost records the established standard cost for purchased parts and material used in the assembly on the appropriate line of the bill of material. Cost also notes the established total dollar standard costs for manufactured parts and lower-level subassemblies used in the assembly and posts them on the appropriate line of the bill of material.

As with manufactured parts, there are as many theories for determining standard labor hours for an assembly as there are graduate industrial engineers and assembly department supervisors. It is recommended that a knowledgeable person estimate hours to assemble for the first-cut standard assembly hour figure and note the estimate on the bill of material. Cost can then add the standard costs for each line item and the assembly labor hours extended by the appropriate labor and burden hourly rate to arrive at the standard cost for the complete assembly.

Standard Direct Labor Hourly Rate

Direct labor is labor applied directly to creating the product. The direct labor work force is the cadre of people that spend the bulk of their time creating the product. Direct labor people also spend some portion of their workday on indirect labor functions, such as training, cleanup of their workplace, company meetings, lunch, and coffee breaks. As a rule of thumb, 80 percent of the workday is spent on direct labor creating the product, and 20 percent is spent on indirect labor functions.

Attempting to record actual labor dollars using the actual operator labor rate would be cumbersome and is really not necessary. At standard-setting time, which normally follows budget-setting time, it is recommended that anticipated departmental direct labor hourly rates or a factory-wide direct labor hourly rate be calculated and established as a standard direct labor hourly rate. This is calculated by dividing the total budgeted direct labor dollar amount by the budgeted head count equivalent in hours.

Standard Burden Rate

Factory burden, sometimes called overhead, includes all indirect factory expenses: wages and salaries of all manufacturing function people other than the direct labor portion of the direct labor work force; fringe benefits; the portion of rent, power, gas, water, and other utilities allocated to the factory floor space; expendable tools; supplies such as cutting oil, glue, paint, and forms; freight in; sustaining engineering; and other such expenses. Your CPA can help you determine the content of factory burden.

The factory burden or overhead rate is the ratio of indirect expense to direct labor; it can be a factory-wide or a departmental rate. The burden rate is established at standard- or budget-setting time and normally remains constant until the next budget cycle. It is calculated by dividing the total dollar amount of budgeted factory indirect expense by the total dollar amount of budgeted direct labor; for example, indirect expense = $100, direct labor = $75, burden rate = 100/75 = 133%.

Standard Labor and Burden Hourly Rate

The standard labor and burden hourly rate can be departmental or factory-wide. It is calculated by adding the standard direct labor hourly rate to the standard direct labor hourly rate extended by the standard burden rate. For example, standard direct labor hourly rate = $5, standard burden rate = 133%, and so standard labor and burden hourly rate = $5 + $5(1.33) = $11.65.

Material Charges to Work Orders

Material for manufactured-part work orders is drawn from the stockroom via stock requisitions, Figure 16-21, which note the unit of measure quantity, the type of material, and the specific work order it was charged to. After the transaction is posted to the inventory record, the stock requisition is forwarded to cost.

The quantities of parts and material initially picked and kitted for an assembly work order are noted on the work order pick copy of the bill of material. When the initial pick is completed, a copy of the picked bill of material is forwarded to cost. As shortages are filled or, for whatever reason, additional parts and material are required to complete an assembly work order, they are drawn from the stockroom via stock requisitions that note the work order they are charged to. The stock requisitions are forwarded to cost after the inventory record is posted.

Labor Charges to Work Orders

Labor hours to the closest 0.1 hour are posted to the time record stamp on the work order or on a time record log by the operators performing the work. Completed work orders and time record logs are forwarded to cost.

Completed Work Orders

When work orders are completed, the actual quantity completed and transferred to stock or to another work order is verified by the stockroom on the transfer stamp on the work order. Completed work orders are forwarded to cost after the inventory record is posted.

STANDARD COST ACCOUNTING PROCESS

The essence of the standard cost accounting process is that all labor, parts, and material transactions to open work orders are debited or charged to WIP. Offsetting credits are to stockroom inventory and payroll. All debits or charges stay in WIP until the end product is sold or transferred to finished goods. Cost files transaction source documents in individual open work order suspense files.

When work orders are completed, they are forwarded to cost. Cost calculates the standard cost dollars and variance dollars of parts actually transferred. *Variance dollars* are the difference between the total dollar amount of labor, parts, and material charged to the work order and the standard cost dollar value of parts actually completed and transferred. Cost then credits WIP with the total dollar amount charged to the work order and debits or charges the standard cost dollar value of parts actually completed to finished goods, cost of sales, the next higher level work order, or whatever account the completed parts were transferred to. The difference between the WIP credit and the standard cost debit is debited or credited to variance. The variance debit or credit is recorded on the current accounting period income statement as a period cost or credit to profit. Cost then generates and issues variance reports.

At the close of an accounting period, burden variance is calculated. *Burden variance* is the difference between the actual dollar amount of factory indirect expense incurred during the period and the dollar amount of burden applied to WIP at the standard labor and burden hourly rate. Assume a burden rate of 133 percent and a direct labor hourly rate of $5.00. One hour of direct labor applied to WIP will apply $6.65 of burden to WIP: $5.00(133%) = $6.65. Assume that 100 direct labor hours are applied to WIP and $500 actual factory indirect expense is incurred. Then $665 would be applied to WIP: $6.65(100 hours) = $665. Burden variance is $165: $665 − $500 = $165. Burden variance is period-costed to cost of goods sold as overapplied or underapplied burden. In this example, the $165 is overapplied burden. More burden was applied to WIP than was incurred, and the variance is a credit to COGS. Underapplied burden, less burden applied to WIP than incurred, is a debit to COGS.

To illustrate the cost accounting process, we will use the standard cost accounting flowchart, Figure 13-5.

When cost receives their copy of a manufactured-part work order, they create an open work order suspense file. When cost receives the pick copy of an assembly work order bill of material, cost uses the assembly standard cost bill of material to calculate the standard cost of the initial picked parts and material. Cost debits the initial pick standard cost to WIP and credits stockroom inventory. Cost then establishes an open assembly work order suspense file.

As stock requisitions are received, cost debits WIP and credits the stockroom for the standard cost of the stock requisitions. Posted stock requisitions are placed in open work order suspense files.

Time records received by cost are extended by appropriate labor and burden hourly rates. WIP is debited, payroll is credited. Posted time records are placed in open work order suspense files.

When the completed work order is received, cost uses the completed work order, the pick copy of the assembly work order bill of material, stock requisitions, and time records to calculate the actual cost of completing the work order and posts the results to the cost history record. Cost then credits WIP, debits the transferred-to account, and debits or credits variance. Cost generates and issues variance reports.

Completed work orders, the pick copy of assembly work order bills of material, stock requisitions, and time records are all filed in a closed work order file, which is an audit trail.

The cost accounting process for purchased parts and material is covered on the bottom of Figure 13-5. It is suggested that cost accounting for

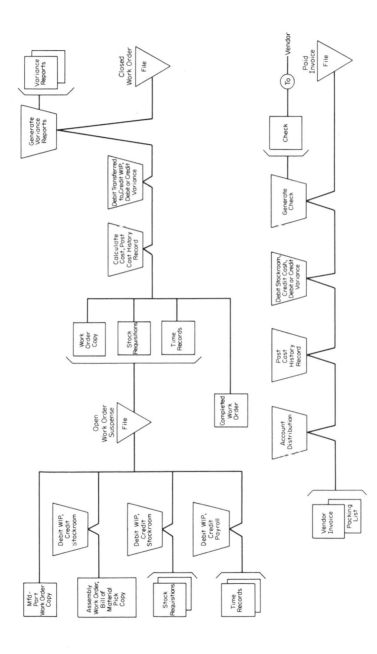

FIGURE 13-5 Standard cost accounting flowchart

purchased items be performed by accounts payable. When the account distribution of vendor invoice charges is made and the invoice is paid, accounts payable posts the cost history record, debits stockroom inventory with the standard cost of the parts or material, credits cash, and debits or credits variance with the difference between the stockroom debit and the actual cost of the parts or material. Freight in, tax, and other expenses are debited to appropriate expense accounts.

COST HISTORY RECORD

To illustrate the use of the cost history record and variance calculations, we will use a manufactured-part and a purchased-part example. The first example is a manufactured part, Figure 13-6.

At standard-setting time, cost establishes the standard labor and burden hourly rate and the standard cost for purchased parts and material. Cost uses these data to establish the standard cost data, noted in the blocks on the bottom of the form:

Cost History Record												
Lot — Date Comp.	Qty. Xfr'd.	Labor						Material			Total		
		Std. Hrs.	Act. Hrs.	Var. Hrs.	Std. $	Act. $	Var. $	Std. $	Act. $	Var. $	Std. $	Act. $	Var. $
-001 2-1-80	10	15.0	18.5	(3.5)	174.80	215.53	(40.73)	30.00	36.00	(6.00)	204.80	251.53	(46.73)

Date 1-1-80	Date _____	Date _____	M	Description: MANUFACTURED PART	Part #
Std. Hrs. 1.5	Std. Hrs. _____	Std. Hrs. _____			∿
Std.Lab.$ 17.48	Std.Lab.$ _____	Std. Lab.$_____	A		
Std.Mat'l$ 3.00	Std.Mat'l$ _____	Std.Mat'l$_____		Std. Unit of Measure:	
Std.Ttl.$ 20.48	Std.Ttl.$ _____	Std.Ttl.$ _____	P	1.5 INCHES	

FIGURE 13-6   Manufactured-part cost history record

Date: Date the standard was set—in the example, January 1, 1980.

Standard Hours: Estimated by a knowledgeable person—in the example, 1.5 hours per piece.

Standard Labor $: The standard labor dollars per piece are calculated by extending the standard labor and burden hourly rate by the standard hours—in the example, $11.65(1.5) = $17.48.

Standard Material $: Standard material dollars for manufactured parts are calculated by extending the standard cost per unit of measure by the gross unit of measure quantity—in the example, $2.00(1.5) = $3.00.

Standard material dollars for assembly cost history records are the total standard cost of all parts, material, and lower-level subassemblies used on the assembly. They are detailed on the standard cost working copy of the bill of material.

Standard Total $: Standard total dollars are the sum of standard labor dollars and standard material dollars—in the example, $17.48 + $3.00 = $20.48.

Gross Unit of Measure Quantity: Estimate by a knowledgeable person of the gross material required per piece—in the example, 1.5 inches. This block is not used on assembly cost history records.

Cost history is accumulated in the body of the cost history form.

Lot–Date Complete: Lot number and date the lot was completed—in the example, lot 001 was completed on February 1, 1980.

Quantity Transferred: The actual quantity transferred, taken from the stock transfer stamp on the completed work order, verified by the stockroom—in the example, 10 pieces.

Under the labor heading:

Standard Hours: The quantity transferred extended by the standard hours per piece—in the example, 10(1.5) = 15.0.

Actual Hours: The actual number of hours recorded on the time record stamp on the completed work order—in the example, 18.5 hours were logged on the completed work order.

Variance Hours: The difference between standard and actual hours—in the example, 18.5 − 15.0 = (3.5). The parentheses indicate negative variance. Negative variance occurs when actual exceeds standard. Positive variance occurs when actual is less than standard.

Standard $: Standard labor dollars. Standard labor dollars are calculated by extending the standard labor dollars per piece by the quantity transferred—in the example, $17.48(10) = $174.80.

Actual $: Actual labor dollars. Actual labor dollars are calculated by extending the actual number of hours by the standard labor and burden hourly rate—in the example, 18.5($11.65) = $215.53.

Variance $: Labor variance dollars. Labor variance dollars are the difference between actual and standard labor dollars. In the example, $215.53 − $174.80 = ($40.73).

Under the material heading:

Standard $: Standard material dollars. Standard material dollars are calculated by extending the quantity transferred by the standard material dollars per piece—in the example, 10($3.00) = $30.00.

Actual $: Actual material dollars. Actual material dollars are calculated by extending the quantity of material charged to the work order through stock requisitions by the standard material dollars per piece—in the example, 18 inches($2.00) = $36.00.

Actual material dollars for assembly cost history records is the standard cost of all parts and materials charged to the work order via the pick copy of the work order bill of material and subsequent stock requisitions.

Under the total heading:

Standard $: Total standard dollars is the sum of standard labor and standard material dollars—in the example, $174.80 + $30.00 = $204.80.

Actual $: Total actual dollars is the sum of actual labor and material dollars—in the example, $215.53 + $36.00 = $251.53.

Variance $: Total variance dollars is the difference between total standard and actual dollars. In the example, $215.53 − $204.80 = ($46.73).

Next, a purchased-part cost history record, Figure 13-7, will be examined. The standard cost of $0.65 was set on January 1, 1980: 125 pieces were invoiced against purchase order 123 on February 1, 1980, at $0.75 each. Total standard dollars of $81.25 are calculated by extending the 125 pieces received by the standard cost of $0.65 per part: 125($0.65) = $81.25. Total actual dollars of $93.75 are calculated by extending the 125 pieces received by the invoiced cost of $0.75 per part: 125($0.75) = $93.75.

Lot	Qty.	Labor						Material			Total		
Date Comp.	Xfr'd.	Std. Hrs.	Act. Hrs.	Var. Hrs.	Std. $	Act. $	Var. $	Std. $	Act. $	Var. $	Std. $	Act. $	Var. $
123 2-1-80	125							0.75			81.25	93.75	(12.50)

Cost History Record

Date 1-1-80	Date	Date		Description:	Part #
Std. Hrs.	Std. Hrs.	Std. Hrs.	M	PURCHASED PART	
Std.Lab.$	Std.Lab.$	Std. Lab.$	A		∿
Std.Mat'l$ 0.65	Std.Mat'l$	Std.Mat'l$	Ⓟ	Std. Unit of Measure:	
Std.Ttl.$	Std.Ttl.$	Std.Ttl.$			

FIGURE 13-7   Purchased-part cost history record

The ($12.50) negative variance is the difference between total standard and actual dollars.

VARIANCE REPORTS

Although it is possible to issue a myriad of variance reports, three key ones are recommended: labor hour variance, work order material variance, and purchased parts and material variance.

Labor Hour Variance Report

A typical labor hour variance report is shown in Figure 13-8. Depending on the size of the work force, labor hour variance reports can include the entire factory, all assembly by assembly department, all manufacturing by manufacturing department, and, in extremely sophisticated operations, individual operators.

In the example, actual labor hours, standard labor hours, and variance labor hours are noted for each month. A positive or negative actual vari-

		Jan	Feb	Mar	Apr	May	Jun	Jul	Aug	Sep	Oct	Nov	Dec
	ASSEMBLY HOURS Variance Report									Date 12-31-79			
Actual		115	124	132	142	154	168	181	187	196	200	190	189
Standard		100	110	120	130	140	150	160	170	180	190	200	213
Variance		(15)	(14)	(12)	(14)	(18)	(18)	(21)	(17)	(16)	(10)	10	24

FIGURE 13-8   Labor hour variance report

ance trend line is plotted. Negative variance occurs when actual hours exceed standard. Positive variance occurs when actual hours are less than standard.

The goal of variance improvement established for manufacturing management is also noted.

In the example, the actual trend line improved, although it did not quite reach the goal during the early part of the year. During the summer months it turned negative, but in the early fall it improved significantly and ended up better than the goal at the end of the year.

The labor hour variance report is probably the best management tool available for diagnosing the relative health or weakness of a factory. A negative variance trend such as that experienced during midyear in the example can be a symptom of any of a number of possible problems in the factory: third-party activity, poor supervision, shortage of parts and material, lack of training, improper tools and equipment, and so on. A positive variance trend, particularly if there are departmental labor hour variance reports, should be studied. Managers experiencing favorable or positive variance trends should be observed to see what they are doing right so that other supervisors can be urged to emulate their winning programs.

Work Order Material Variance

Because all parts and material transactions are at standard cost, material variance tracks the actual quantities used versus standard quantities. Negative material variance is another name for scrap on manufactured-part work orders or inaccurate counts on assembly work order picks and stock requisition picks.

Purchased Parts and Material Variance

The trend of purchased parts and material variance provides a good measure of purchasing management performance and is a key parameter for pricing decisions. If mandatory wage and price controls are invoked, it provides the justification for increasing prices to cover increased costs of purchased parts and material.

Other Variance

Tracking labor dollar variance is not recommended. It would provide the same relative trend data as the labor hour report. Hours are easier to calculate and relate directly to an excessive direct labor head count.

Tracking total work order dollar variance is also not recommended. Because total variance is a combination of labor and material variance, it is difficult to diagnose symptoms or causes of positive or negative trends.

SEMISTANDARD COST INVENTORY COST SYSTEM

A full standard cost system makes sense in a relatively large ongoing situation with several manufacturing or assembly departments and a relatively broad product line.

In a start-up or smaller ongoing situation, a semistandard cost system is appropriate when an inventory asset on the balance sheet is desired. In this system, purchased parts and material are washed through an inventory account. Direct labor and indirect factory expense are period-costed. The system is relatively simple to set up and operate.

At standard-setting time, working copies of bills of material are used to establish the purchased parts and material standard cost dollar value for each product. It is desirable, but not mandatory, that cost history records for each purchased part and material unit of measure be established.

If cost history records are established, the cost accounting process is as shown on the bottom of Figure 13-5, with the standard cost of all parts and material purchased in a given accounting period debited to inventory. Inventory is credited and cost of sales is debited with the product standard cost for each product invoiced during the accounting period. It is recommended that a k factor, established as a judgment call, be applied on top of product standard cost to compensate for material usage variance. Without the k factor, book inventory will tend to become overstated over time, and this will result in an inventory write-down equal to actual material variance against profit when a physical inventory is taken.

If cost history records are not established, the actual invoice value of all parts and material purchased in a given accounting period is debited to inventory. Inventory is credited and cost of sales is debited with product standard cost for each product invoiced during the accounting period. In this case, the recommended k factor should include an amount to cover purchased material variance as well as usage variance to avoid overstating book inventory.

14

CASH
MANAGEMENT

The survival of your company is highly dependent on your ability to manage cash. Managing cash is often a mysterious and awesome experience for the start-up entrepreneur. When you worked for a large company, someone else worried about managing cash. All you had to do was live within the confines of your departmental budget. Now that you are the cash manager, every decision you make will be overshadowed by its effect on cash. If decision A will tend to put you in a negative cash position and decision A simply must happen, you will need to find and make an offsetting decision B to restore cash to a positive position. Regardless of how difficult and unpleasant cash decisions may be, they must be made and made promptly.

It is quite possible and probable that making decision A may only cause a short-term cash crunch. If you can figure out a way to stretch your cash for a few days, weeks, or months, an offsetting decision B may not be necessary. This book suggests several ways or techniques to float vendors or creditors. Floating cash, otherwise known as using someone else's cash in lieu of yours, is perfectly legitimate and has, in recent years, become an accepted practice in industry. If your decision A realistically means a short-term cash shortage that can reasonably be offset by a short-term float program, the wise course is to proceed. If, on the other hand, the decision to invoke a short-term float program will only defer decision B, do not succumb. Making tough cash decisions is difficult, unpleasant, and hard management work. Making them will prove to be very rewarding in the long run, when your company has become self-sustaining with adequate cash. By definition, successful ongoing manufacturing-company entrepreneurs have mastered the art of managing cash.

A common misperception regarding cash is that cash is another word for profit. Many people erroneously think that profitable companies have no cash problems. They reason that if $X in profit was generated in a given accounting period, then $X in cash was also accumulated. Such is not normally the case. Cash and profit are distinctly different. About the only thing cash and profit have in common is that their numerical values are preceded by dollar signs. Cash is wampum, or a commodity that is paid to your company by customers for your product. Cash is also a commodity used by your company as wampum to pay for parts, material, labor, and services. Profit is the residual dollar-value difference between the dollar value of net sales and the dollar value of costs and expenses during a given accounting period. There is only an extremely remote possibility that profit and net cash will come close to being equal in a given accounting period. If they are exactly equal, it is a very unlikely coincidence or a fluke.

This chapter explores the difference between cash and profit, how to plan cash needs, and how to defer cash payments using a strategy or technique called *cash float*.

THE DIFFERENCE BETWEEN CASH AND PROFIT

A hypothetical example of profitable and fast-growing ABC, Inc., will illustrate the disparity between cash and profit and will also provide some insights into the income statement and the cash-flow projection. We will use a pro forma income statement and cash-flow projection, Figures 14-1 and 14-2, for the same year.

ABC, Inc. Proforma Income Statement ($000)

	Jan	Feb	Mar	Apr	May	Jun	Jul	Aug	Sep	Oct	Nov	Dec	Total Year
Net Sales:													
Product A	100	110	120	130	140	150	160	170	180	190	200	210	1,860
Product B	-	-	-	-	-	-	-	-	10	20	30	40	100
Total	100	110	120	130	140	150	160	170	190	210	230	250	1,960
Cost of Sales	40	44	48	52	56	60	64	68	76	84	92	100	784
Gross Margin	60	66	72	78	84	90	96	102	114	126	138	150	1,176
Expenses:													
Marketing	15	15	15	15	15	15	20	25	30	30	30	25	250
R & D	15	15	15	20	20	20	20	20	20	15	15	15	210
G & A	15	15	15	15	15	15	20	20	20	20	15	15	200
Total	45	45	45	50	50	50	60	65	70	65	60	55	660
Net Before Tax Profit	15	21	27	28	34	40	36	37	44	61	78	95	516

FIGURE 14-1   ABC, Inc., pro forma income statement

	Jan	Feb	Mar	Apr	May	Jun	Jul	Aug	Sep	Oct	Nov	Dec	Total Year
ABC, Inc. Proforma Cash Flow Projection											($000)		
Receipts: Collected													
Receivables	70	80	90	100	110	120	130	140	150	160	170	180	1,500
Loan Proceeds	65	·	·	50	·	·	70	·	·	15	·	·	200
Total Cash In	135	80	90	150	110	120	200	140	150	175	170	180	1,700
Material:													
Product A	39	42	45	48	51	54	57	60	63	66	69	72	666
Product B	·	·	·	·	·	3	6	9	12	15	18	21	84
Total	39	42	45	48	51	57	63	69	75	81	87	93	750
Direct Labor:													
Product A	8	9	10	11	12	13	14	15	16	17	18	19	162
Product B							1	2	3	4	5	6	21
Total	8	9	10	11	12	13	15	17	19	21	23	25	183
Tooling Product B	·	·	·	·	10	10	10	10	·	·	·	·	40
Salaries	25	25	25	25	25	25	35	35	35	35	35	35	360
Expenses	25	25	25	30	30	30	30	35	40	35	30	25	360
Total Cash Out	97	101	105	114	128	135	153	166	169	172	175	178	1693
Net Cash	38	(21)	(15)	36	(18)	(15)	47	(26)	(19)	3	(5)	2	·
Cumulative Cash	38	17	2	38	20	15	52	26	7	10	5	7	·

FIGURE 14-2   ABC, Inc., pro forma cash-flow projection

It is common practice to round off figures on accounting statements to the nearest dollar. Larger companies often round off figures to the nearest thousand dollars and note "dollars in thousands" or ($000) on the statement. Extremely large companies round off figure on financial statements to the closest million dollars. In Figures 14-1 and 14-2, the numbers have been rounded off to the nearest thousand dollars, as signified by the ($000) appended to the statements.

In business vernacular, a "K" after a dollar figure indicates that the figure is in thousands. An "M" after a dollar figure indicates that the figure is in millions. For example, $15K is interpreted as $15,000 or fifteen kilobucks; $8M is interpreted as $8,000,000 and is called eight megabucks.

The figures for each month on each line of the pro forma income statement and cash-flow projection must be supported by valid assumptions. In real life, your banker or other source of working capital will thoroughly test your assumptions. Their decision to grant the loan or provide the funds is, to a large extent, dependent upon their perception of the validity or reality of your assumptions.

Pro Forma Income Statement

Pro forma income statements prepared for planning purposes take the form of a chart of monthly condensed income statements, as depicted in

Figure 14-1. The following assumptions for each line item of the ABC pro forma income statement also include some explanation of the line items and how the figures are derived.

Net Sales   Net sales for existing product *A* are projected to increase $10K per month across the year. Initial shipment or sale of new product *B* is planned in September at $10K. Sales of new product *B* are projected to increase $10K per month for the balance of the year.

Cost of Sales   ABC uses a standard cost system. The standard cost of existing product *A* is 75 percent material and 25 percent labor and burden. New product *B* is similar in many respects to existing product *A*, and so standard cost for new product *B* is also projected at 75 percent material and 25 percent labor and burden.

Gross Margin   Gross margin is the difference between net sales and cost of sales. The projected net selling price for both products less standard cost is projected to provide a 60 percent gross margin ratio.

Marketing Expense   Marketing expense is projected at $15K per month through June. Plans to hire additional people in the third quarter and heavy promotional expense for new product *B* account for the peak September, October, and November figures. Marketing expense is expected to level off at $25K per month starting in December.

R&D Expense   R&D expense is projected at $15K per month for the first quarter. Subcontract tool and test equipment design for new product *B* is projected to add $5K per month April through September. R&D expense is expected to return to its normal $15K per month in October.

G&A Expense   G&A expense is projected at $15K per month through June. The additional $5K per month July through October is to cover additional travel and entertainment to be incurred by people other than marketing in launching new product *B*.

Total Expense   Total expense is the sum of marketing, R&D, and G&A expenses.

Net Before-Tax Profit   NBT is the difference between gross margin and total expense. Pro forma income statements normally do not include other income or expense or taxes.

Cash-Flow Projection

ABC, Inc., is an ongoing company with a good track record of profitability and growth. ABC's president has discussed the growth plans for existing product *A* and the planned addition of new product *B* with ABC's banker. Based on ABC's track record, the bank has tentatively agreed to increase ABC's credit line by an additional $250K maximum subject to the bank's review of and concurrence with the assumptions underlying ABC's pro forma income statement and cash-flow projection.

Cash Receipts   Cash receipts are based on net sales with 90 days in receivables, which is the average number of days' sales in receivables ABC is currently experiencing. The collected receivables of $70K projected in January are the $70K of net sales invoiced the previous October. As you will discover, a cash-flow projection is a cut-and-try proposition. When cash receipts from operations are realistically projected, expenses such as those for launching new product *B* must be scheduled within the confines of the available credit line. In this case, the cut-and-try exercise indicated that using $65K of the tentative credit line in January, $50K in April, $70K in June, and $15K in October would enable new product *B* to be brought on stream for initial shipment in September.

Total Cash In   Total cash in reflects incoming cash from all sources— in this illustration, cash receipts from receivables and proceeds from additional loans.

Material   ABC's payment policy is 30 days. Expenditures for material for existing product *A* reflect this payment policy. In the case of material for new product *B*, plans call for the initial material to be received in May, and the first cash expenditure is projected for June. Material for both products reflects standard cost.

Direct Labor   Direct labor is normally projected separately from other salary expense because it is quite volatile. Direct labor for both products reflects standard cost and lead time setback.

Tooling and Test Equipment Purchases of tooling and test equipment required to manufacture new product *B* are projected at $10K per month May through August.

Salaries All salaries other than direct labor are projected at $25K per month through June. The $35K salary expense projected for July through the balance of the year covers the additional marketing people and indirect manufacturing people required to launch new product *B*.

Expenses The $25K expense level projected for the first quarter and the month of December reflect normal monthly expense levels. The additional expenses projected in April through November reflect additional expense to launch new product *B*, including subcontracted design of tooling and test equipment, marketing expense, and extra travel, as discussed in the income statement assumptions.

Total Cash Out Total cash out projected for each month is the monthly total of material, direct labor, tooling and test equipment, salary, and expenses.

Net Cash Net cash is the difference between total cash in and total cash out. If total cash in exceeds total cash out, net cash will be positive. If total cash out exceeds total cash in, net cash will be negative. Negative net cash is indicated by parentheses.

Cumulative Cash Cumulative cash is calculated by adding the monthly net cash figures across the year. That is, the positive $38K for January added to the negative ($21K) for February gives the positive $17K cumulative February figure. Adding the negative ($15K) for March gives $2K positive cumulative cash for March. Adding the positive $36K for April gives a positive $38K cumulative for April, and so on. The name of the game in constructing cash-flow projections is to plan cash in and cash out so that cumulative cash is always a positive figure.

The name of the game in managing cash is to control cash receipts and cash expenditures so that your bank account is never overdrawn. If, for some reason, an overdraft for a short period of time is unavoidable, contact your banker in advance to arrange for the bank to cover it. Most banks will cover an occasional small overdraft.

Analysis of the ABC Example

The large disparity that can exist beteeen cash and profit is well illustrated in the ABC example. The pro forma income statement projects a before-tax profit every month and $516K NBT profit for the year. The pro forma cash-flow projection includes additional loans of $200K. In other words, while projecting $516K NBT from operations, ABC projects a $200K cash deficit from operations. The author has calculated that without the new product *B* program, profit would have been $576K, or $60K higher than with the new product *B* program. Year-end cash without the new product *B* program would have been a positive $147K instead of the negative $200K with the new product *B* program.

The importance of cash planning and cash management cannot be overemphasized. The cash-flow projection is the management tool to determine what your company can afford to do and when it can afford to do it. Managing cash to the plan means the difference between failure and success. Unplanned, and therefore unmanaged, negative cash flow can sink your company into failure and oblivion in a matter of a few weeks.

Cash-flow projections for start-up companies and ongoing companies that are growing rapidly are similar to the ABC example. It is normal for a start-up company to experience planned and managed negative cash flow for several months until monthly cash in exceeds monthly cash out. It is also not unusual for high-growth ongoing profitable companies to experience periods of planned and managed negative cash flow similar to the ABC example.

CASH FLOAT

The ABC example illustrates the short-term need for cash above the level produced from operations to finance periods of rapid growth and to finance the launching of major new products. Short-term cash needs can be met by borrowing. They can also be met by using funds of others to provide the additional inventory needed to boost production to a higher level and to provide the wherewithal to launch a new product program. Using funds of others is called *cash float*. Methods of floating cash include a program called *dated payables* and the use of moonlighters.

Dated Payables

As discussed in the accounts payable section of Chapter 12, "Accounting," it is possible to float vendors by simply delaying payment. This process is a form of dated payables that does not cost you anything. Assuming that your vendors are confident that your company is viable and will continue to grow profitably, it is possible to date payables for the total time period required to build up inventory, ship the product, and collect the receivables. This technique can be used to finance a higher production rate for an existing product or to finance the initial production lot of a new product.

The process is quite simple. First, make a conservative cash-flow projection to determine the dollar amount to be floated and the length of time it needs to be floated. The next step is to meet with your vendors for a frank discussion of your needs to float this dollar amount and how long you need to float it. It is obviously not practical to negotiate an extended dated payable arrangement with all vendors. The 80-20 rule will probably apply, which means that you should be able to float 80 percent of the dollars you need with something less than 20 percent of your vendors.

Extended dated payable arrangements with vendors usually end up as short-term promissory notes at an agreed-to interest rate at the dollar level you require and the time interval you need for a specific list of commodities purchased on a single purchase order. Most vendors will settle for an interest rate equal to what they have to pay for their money, which is probably very close to what you would have to pay. If the worst happens and you simply do not have the cash to pay off the notes when they are due, the probability of your vendors extending them is quite high.

Moonlighters

The proper use of moonlighters enables you to float a significant portion of the cost of a new product development program. You accomplish this by creating a cadre of moonlighters who have the technical skills your new product program requires. Most, but certainly not all, technical people employed by large companies enjoy an occasional moonlight job to provide some extra money for a new TV set or, in the case of a large project, an automobile. Most, but again not all, moonlighters are willing to wait some weeks or months to be paid, provided that they are confident that you will eventually come through. It is possible to float practically everything needed for the basic product design. It is also possible to float the actual construction of engineering models, prototypes, and even an initial production run using moonlighting technicians and dated payables for parts and material.

Deferred Professional Start-Up Services

In a start-up situation, you will need the services of attorneys or legal counsel and a certified public accounting firm. One- or two-partner law firms and accounting firms are suggested for a number of reasons: their fees are generally lower than those of larger firms, they are more flexible, they are more familiar and at home with smaller companies such as yours, and they are more amenable to deferred compensation for the start-up services they perform for you. Use your pro forma income statement to make the case that you are planning a profitable and long-enduring business. Use your pro forma cash-flow projection to make the case that you cannot afford the cash outlay for their start-up services until your monthly cash flow turns positive. Negotiate deferred payment at no charge if possible or at a nominal carrying charge. Some firms will provide start-up services in exchange for a few shares of stock.

PART SIX
DOCUMENTATION

The two chapters in Part 6—"Database" and "Working Documents"—provide formats and descriptions of fifty forms used by manufacturing companies. They include suggestions about which forms to use in a start-up situation, which are needed in larger ongoing operations, and which are optional.

CHAPTER 15: DATABASE

This chapter provides suggested formats for, and a discussion of the need for, use of, and suggested management policies regarding, documents that are permanent or subject to very infrequent change.

CHAPTER 16: WORKING DOCUMENTS

This chapter provides suggested formats for documents that trigger action steps, that record transactions, that are planning tools, or that are used to prepare "to do" lists. It also discusses the need for, use of, and suggested management policies to control the proliferation of paperwork.

15
DATABASE

The database includes records that are permanent or subject to very infrequent change.

The ten documents included in this chapter are the ones directly concerned with day-to-day operation of the business. Some of them define the product so that it can be manufactured. Others are reference documents used by different functions. There are other database documents, including payroll and personnel records, journals and ledgers of the general accounting system, and other such records, that are not included.

No one is comfortable contemplating a disaster, such as fire, flood, or theft. Loss of any company data for whatever reason will cause problems. Loss of database documents could well kill the company. There is a simple method for creating a disaster file of precious database documents: simply instruct whoever issues newly released or revised database documents into the system to make an extra copy and give it to you. Take it home and put it in a large box. In the event of a disaster, you and your partners can sort through the box and readily reconstruct your entire database.

In a start-up situation, the minimum database you will need includes bills of material and engineering drawings. The xmas tree and part number register are recommended from the outset, but they are not mandatory. There are no hard and fast rules on when to add additional documentation to the database. All the documents in this chapter will be needed when you have different individuals performing the different functions of the business.

The need for an accurate, complete, and up-to-date database is obvious. Getting it there is not easy. Keeping it accurate and up-to-date is even more difficult and requires discipline. Most database documents are created and maintained by engineering. By definition, engineers are creative people who absolutely abhor the detail and tedious paperwork associated with creating and maintaining the database. Creativity notwithstanding, it is recommended that you do whatever needs doing to ensure that your database is maintained. Removing errors and updating a neglected database can be very expensive and time-consuming.

This chapter provides a sample format for each database document and a discussion of the need for, use of, and suggested management policies regarding each one.

XMAS TREE

An xmas tree is recommended for each product to picture how the product is structured. All anticipated bills of material should be included.

The shipping assembly includes the final assembly, packaging and packing material, and ancillary items such as the operation and maintenance manual and spare parts, or everything that is shipped to the customer. The final assembly includes the basic assembly and options. Assemblies below the basic or options level are called subassemblies.

It is recommended that the xmas tree be prepared during the new product project planning process. It is used at that juncture to assure that

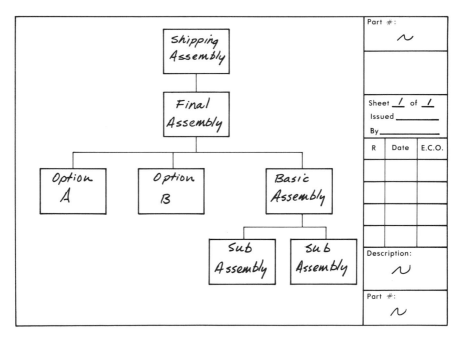

FIGURE 15-1   Xmas tree

		Part #	Description	M A P	Qty		Part #:		
1									
2									
3							Bill of Material		
4							Sheet __ of __ Issued ___		
5							By ___		
6							Rev.	Date	E.C.O.
7									
8									
9									
10									
11							Description:		
12									
13									
14							Part #:		
15									

FIGURE 15-2   Bill of material

the planned documentation package will satisfy the requirements of engineering, marketing, and manufacturing. It is particularly useful in the planning process for estimating the number of bills of material and drawings required, material, parts and labor costs, and so on. It is also useful for indoctrinating new employees in an ongoing business.

BILL OF MATERIAL

The bill of material is a list of everything that is needed to manufacture the assembly it covers: purchased parts, manufactured parts, material, lower-level assemblies, and so on. It is recommended that support documents, such as schematics, test procedures, process specifications, and assembly aids, also be noted on the bill of material for reference purposes. A bill of material should be prepared for each assembly that will be manufactured and stocked as a discrete entity.

Do not allow any function to establish a parts list separate from the bill of material. Everyone who needs a parts list can use the bill of material. If separate parts lists are made, sooner or later they will no longer agree with the bill of material. Significant amounts of energy will be wasted, not only in keeping separate lists up to date with the bill of material, but in trying to discover why they do not agree and who was at fault in causing them to disagree.

Engineering should avoid putting data in the two columns without column headings. This space is for functions that use the bill of material for other purposes.

ENGINEERING DRAWING

It is recommended that engineering drawings be prepared only for unique parts that will be manufactured in-house or outside specifically for your product. Drawings should not be prepared for standard catalog purchased items unless there is some compelling reason for doing so. In this case, it is recommended that only the key specifications or dimensions be noted on the drawing to facilitate receiving inspection.

The use of assembly aids rather than assembly drawings is recommended. Assembly drawings are expensive to generate and maintain and are often not as useful in the assembly process as an equivalent assembly aid. Assembly aids can consist of a model or photographs; if an illustrated parts breakdown is generated for the maintenance manual, the same artwork can serve as an excellent assembly aid.

Part #:
Sheet ___ of ___
Issued _____
By _____

Rev.	Date	E.C.O.

Description:
Part #:

FIGURE 15-3　Engineering drawing

Part Number Register							
Part #	Description	First Used On	M A P	Part #	Description	First Used On	M A P

FIGURE 15-4   Part number register

PART NUMBER REGISTER

The part number register is a sequential, ascending number register of all part numbers that have been assigned and issued. Its primary function is to avoid assigning the same part number to different documents. The first used-on is an audit trail.

Having two series of part numbers is recommended. One series covers parts, material, and assemblies that are covered by a released drawing, specification, or bill of material. Support documents such as schematics, wiring diagrams, test procedures, or process details should have part numbers assigned when they are released. A second series of part numbers is recommended for purchased standard catalog parts or material not covered by a released document. In the early stages of a start-up situation, part numbers for standard purchased catalog parts or material are not really needed. Part numbers for catalog items become useful when there is a separate inventory and stockroom function. They can be assigned when they are needed.

The simplest part number system that is most straightforward, and least expensive to create and maintain consists of sequential ascending numbers starting with number 1. Part number systems that attempt to use the part number to identify different materials, types of part, manu-

Used-On Register			M-A-P	Sheu. ___ of ___	Description:	Part #:
Bill of Material	Description	Qty				

FIGURE 15-5   Used-on register

facturing processes, or other codifications, particularly if they use alpha characters with numerics, tend to get complex and clumsy as the business grows and are almost always subsequently abandoned in favor of a straightforward sequentially ascending system. Part numbers with alpha characters are not compatible with computer-based systems. Additionally, as the business grows, codification systems will consume precious engineering resource time in debating "whether this part should be coded X or Y."

USED-ON REGISTER

The used-on register notes all applications of each issued part number. A used-on register should be created at the same time the part number is assigned. If only one application is noted on a used-on register, the part number is unique. The instant a second application is added to a used-on register, the part number becomes a common part number. Its usage is common to two or more part numbers.

Engineering uses the used-on register in assessing the effect of a change to a given part number on all applications of that part number. It is a key document for the inventory function as it consolidates requirements for common parts. In the start-up situation, the used-on register is not mandatory, but do not wait too long to establish it. It will be needed as the product line expands.

VENDOR PART NUMBER REGISTER

The vendor part number register is an audit trail that aids all functions in identifying catalog items by your company part number. It is particu-

Vendor Part Number Register	Vendor _____	
		Page __ of __
Part #	Vendor Part #	Description

FIGURE 15-6   Vendor part number register

larly useful in receiving because not all vendors will identify their shipment with your part number despite your repeated pleas that they do so.
With the register available, the receiving function can apply your company part number when the catalog item is received to facilitate proper
identification. In the start-up situation, this register is not applicable until
you assign part numbers to catalog items.

Alphabetical Register	
Generic Category_____	
Part #	Description

FIGURE 15-7   Alphabetical register

ALPHABETICAL REGISTER

An alphabetical register is useful when you use a wide variety of types or sizes of the same generic commodity, such as screws, nuts, couplings, plumbing fittings, or electrical components. It serves as a company catalog of types or sizes in the system to avoid releasing the same item into the system under several part numbers.

PRODUCTION ROUTE SHEET

The production route sheet describes and sequences all operations required to fabricate a manufactured part. It also serves as a manufactured-part work order and is used by the production function in scheduling and in physically moving the work order from operation to operation and from department to department.

Normally the last operation is to stock. You should note any special requirements for stocking the parts, such as wrapping them in paper or putting them in egg cartons or plastic bags. It is better to have the people that make the parts package them for storage than to depend on the stockroom to guess what is needed to protect the parts.

			Description:	Part #:
	Production Route Sheet			
Op:	Description	Department		

FIGURE 15-8   Production route sheet

Engineering Change Order							ECO #	
Document #	Revision		Description	Used On	Used On	Used On	Sheet __ of __	
	Prior	New						

Advance Notice		ECO		Effectivity	Field Service Effect
By	Date	By	Date		

Description of Change	Reason for Change

FIGURE 15-9   Engineering change order

As the business grows, some parts normally manufactured in-house will have to be subcontracted because of excessive shop loading or other causes. In this situation, the production route sheet will enable purchasing to provide the correct material, tools, jigs, fixtures, or whatever the subcontractor needs to manufacture the part for you. You do not need production route sheets until you have several people in the machine shop with operators that need guidance or instructions.

ENGINEERING CHANGE ORDER

When a part drawing, specification, schematic, wiring diagram, process detail, or other control or support document can no longer produce a satisfactory product as currently documented, an engineering change is necessary. Analysis or empirical experimentation will determine the change to be made. The document should be annotated to note the change required to convert it to producing satisfactory product.

When the change to be made has been determined, analysis of the effectivity of the change should be made: must or should the change be implemented on all devices in the field? If yes, is a product recall or retrofit required? If a recall is not necessary but the change should be implemented in all existing products, a program should be worked out to accomplish the field retrofit in a timely fashion. If a field retrofit is not required, should the change be made on finished goods in stock not yet shipped? If no, can the existing stock of subassembly or piece parts on order be used? If yes, the change will normally be effective on the next production lot ordered.

If the contemplated change is compatible with all other used-ons, the change may be made, provided that the change can be incorporated in existing devices in the field and in inventory in stock as well as in all new production. The change must be interchangeable backward as well as forward. If the proposed change is not compatible with other used-ons for the document concerned or is not interchangeable backward as well as forward, an engineering change cannot be issued. In this case, a new document noting the requirements for this application should be issued, with the initial used-on being this application. The existing document will not be changed. All applications using the new part will be removed from the used-on register of the existing document.

When the change to be made and the effectivity for the device using the part have been determined, an advance notice of engineering change

Cost History Record													
Lot —Date Comp.	Qty. Xfr'd.	Labor						Material			Total		
		Std. Hrs.	Act. Hrs.	Var. Hrs.	Std. $	Act. $	Var. $	Std. $	Act. $	Var. $	Std. $	Act. $	Var. $

Date _____ Std. Hrs. _____ Std.Lab.$ _____ Std.Mat'l$ _____ Std.Ttl.$ _____	Date _____ Std. Hrs. _____ Std.Lab.$ _____ Std.Mat'l$ _____ Std.Ttl.$ _____	Date _____ Std. Hrs. _____ Std. Lab.$ _____ Std.Mat'l$ _____ Std.Ttl.$ _____	M A P	Description: Std. Unit of Measure:	Part #

FIGURE 15-10   Cost history record

order should be issued. To do this, affix the advance notice stamp, Figure 16-35, on the marked-up document, annotate it, and issue copies to people required to take the action per the determined effectivity. When the advance notice has been issued, the change should be entered in the engineering change order log, Figure 16-8. When you are a start-up company, the advance notice is really as far as you need to go. Put the advance notice on a sepia and use the sepia as your master to make working copies of drawings. You can issue the formal engineering change order at any time. The formal engineering change order is nothing more than an audit trail that really is not needed until you are a larger ongoing company.

COST HISTORY RECORD

When a standard cost inventory cost system is used, the cost history record becomes the audit trail for historical cost data on each issued part number. Use of the cost history record is discussed in depth in Chapter 13, "Inventory Cost Systems."

16
WORKING
DOCUMENTS

Working documents either cause or are the result of an action step taken by someone. They record transactions. They are planning documents. They are "to do" lists. They are running or perpetual records. They all have a finite useful life. Some are discarded and others end up in a closed file as an audit trail. All working documents that are necessary to enter a customer order, plan inventory requirements, manufacture parts, assemble the product, ship the product, and properly record costs are included.

In a start-up situation, the minimum set of working documents should include the purchase order, purchase order log, commitment log, invoice, packing list, invoice log, and sales order log. The booking-sales forecast, master schedule, stock requisition log, stock transfer log, time record log, and quotation forms are not mandatory but are recommended from the outset. There are no hard-and-fast rules on when to add additional working documents to the system. It is recommended that the need for additional working documents becomes acute before management authorizes their creation and use. Working documents require people to work them.

This chapter provides a sample format and a discussion of the need for, use of, and suggested management policy for each working document.

PURCHASE ORDER

The purchase order is a contract between your company and a vendor. In a start-up situation, it is also the on-order record. The purchase order form also serves as a purchase requisition. A separate purchase requisition form is not necessary. Its use is covered in Chapter 4, "Purchasing."

Purchase Order							
Vendor:					P.O. #: _____		
					Date _____		
Terms:	F.O.B.	Re-Sale		Ship Via:			
		Taxable					
Item	Quantity	Commodity		Price		Per	Extension
					Total		

If re-sale checked above, all items on this order are for re-sale # _____	Requested Delivery:	Promised Delivery
Requisitioned by: Date:		
Approved: Date		
Phone ☐ Written ☐	By: _____	

FIGURE 16-1   Purchase order

PURCHASE ORDER LOG

The purchase order log is a log of all purchase orders placed in sequentially ascending purchase order number sequence. It is used to avoid assigning the same purchase order number to two or more purchase orders and as a cross reference if purchase orders are filed in alphabetical order by vendor.

Purchase Order Log			
P.O. #	Vendor	Date	

FIGURE 16-2   Purchase order log

COMMITMENT LOG

The commitment log is a management tool to help control or manage cash. As purchase orders are placed, the rounded-off total value of each order is posted in the month column in which you anticipate making payment. It is used to provide data on the cash required to pay for outstanding purchases in future months.

Commitment Log

P.O. #	Jan	Feb	Mar	Apr	May	Jun	Jul	Aug	Sep	Oct	Nov	Dec

FIGURE 16-3   Commitment log

INVOICE

The invoice is an itemized statement of the dollar value due your company covering a shipment to a customer in response to a customer purchase order.

Invoice					
Invoice # _____				Date _____	
Sold To:			Ship To:		
Your Order # _____			Sales Order # _____		
Quantity Ordered	Quantity Shipped	Description	Price	Extension	
Shipped Via:_____				Sub-Total	
Reference # _____				Tax	
F.O.B. _____ Terms _____				Shipping Charge	
				Total	

FIGURE 16-4   Invoice

PACKING LIST

The packing list is a duplicate of the invoice with the price and other charges omitted. It is enclosed with the shipment. It is used by the customer to identify the shipment and as a record that it was received.

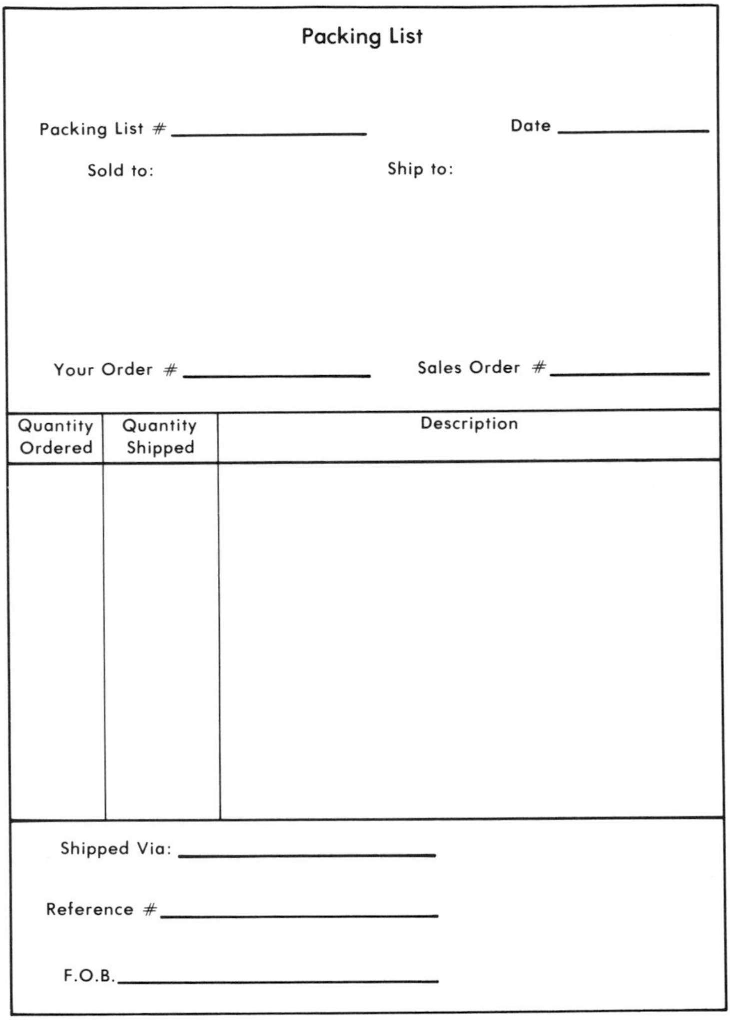

FIGURE 16-5   Packing list

INVOICE LOG

The invoice log is a sequentially ascending number log of all invoices issued. It is used to avoid assigning the same invoice number to two or more invoices and as an audit trail.

Invoice Log					Sales Representative
Invoice #	Invoice Date	Sales Order #	Customer P.O. #	Customer/Institution	Sales Representative

FIGURE 16-6   Invoice log

SALES ORDER LOG

The sales order log is a sequentially ascending number log of all sales orders issued in response to customer purchase orders. It is used to avoid assigning the same sales order number to two or more sales orders, as a cross-reference file, and as an audit trail. The sales order number is the control number used to process the order through the manufacturing, shipment, and invoicing processes.

Sales Order Log					
Sales Order #	S.O. Date	Customer P.O. #	Customer P.O. Date	Customer/Institution	Sales Representative

FIGURE 16-7   Sales order log

ENGINEERING CHANGE ORDER LOG

The engineering change order log is a sequentially ascending number log of all engineering change orders. It is used to avoid assigning the same number to two or more engineering change orders and as an audit trail.

Engineering Change Order Log

ECO #	Document Number	Revision		Description	Advance Notice		ECO		
		Prior	New		By	Date	By	Date	

FIGURE 16-8   Engineering change order log

ENGINEERING PROJECT AUTHORITY

The engineering project authority is a layout of all resources required to conduct a new product development program. It spells out the scope or magnitude of the planned engineering effort in hours and equivalent dollars per month and the total for various types of engineering people, monthly planned project material dollars, and other expense dollars for a new product development program. Key events, such as "mechanical layout review," "tool designs completed," and "engineering model completion," can be listed and scheduled in the month in which they are planned to occur. Approval of the engineering project authority commits the company to the new product project and authorizes expenditures for it.

Engineering Project Authority _____   Description _____

		1	2	3	4	5	6	7	8	9	10	11	12	Total
Mechanical Engineer	Hours													
	$													
Electrical Engineer	Hours													
	$													
Drafting	Hours													
	$													
Technician	Hours													
	$													
Other	Hours													
	$													
Material	$													
Other Expense	$													
Total	Hours													
	$													
Key Events														

			Approved	Date
1. _____	3. _____	Customer Spec. _____	R&D	
		Engineering Spec. _____	Mktg _____	___
2. _____	4. _____	Financial Evaluation _____	Mfg _____	___

FIGURE 16-9   Engineering project authority

FINANCIAL EVALUATION

The financial evaluation is a summary of expected sales, costs, expenses, profit, and investment covering a new product development program. It is used to assess the financial viability of a new product project. It notes how each line item is calculated; for example, line 17, Inventory $, is calculated by dividing line 7, cost of sales, by the current inventory turn ratio.

Financial Evaluation					
EPA _____ Description _____					
			By _____	Date _____	
List Price $_____	Year 1	Year 2	Year 3	___ Years	Total
1. Unit Sales					
2. Net Price $ _____					
3. Net Sales (1x2)					
4. Direct Labor $					
5. Burden (@ %) $					
6. Material $					
7. Cost of Sales (4+5+6)					
8. Gross Profit (3-7)					
9. Sales Expense					
10. G&A Expense					
11. Other Expense					
12. Total Expense (9+10+11)					
13. NBT (8-12)					
14. NBT % (13/3)					
Investment					
15. R&D $					
16. Tooling $					
17. Inventory (7/Turns) $					
18. Receivables (@ % Sales) $					
19. Total Investment (15+16+17+18)					
20. R.O.I. (13/19)					
Approvals:					
Marketing Engineering Manufacturing _____					
By_____ Date____ By_____Date____ By_____Date__ By_____ Date__					

FIGURE 16-10   Financial evaluation

BOOKING-SALES FORECAST

The booking-sales forecast is a projection by product or model of the unit volume of booked customer orders anticipated in future months. It is used in conjunction with existing backlog to prepare the master schedule and the build-ship schedule.

Product/Model	Jan	Feb	Mar	Apr	May	Jun	Jul	Aug	Sep	Oct	Nov	Dec
Booking–Sales Forecast — Date _____												

FIGURE 16-11   Booking-sales forecast

MASTER SCHEDULE

The master schedule is a key manufacturing planning document. It is based on the booking-sales forecast and backlog or finished goods policy and establishes the quantity or volume of product to be manufactured and shipped in future months. The master schedule prepared at budget-setting time is the baseline for the total company yearly budget and financial plan. It is also used in the material requirements planning process, discussed in Chapter 7.

Product _____ Master Schedule Date _____										Backlog/Finished Goods Min: Max:		
Basic Unit	1	2	3	4	5	6	7	8	9	10	11	12
Beginning Backlog												
Book/Sales Forecast												
Available												
Build/Ship												
Ending Backlog												
Option %	1	2	3	4	5	6	7	8	9	10	11	12

FIGURE 16-12 Master schedule

BUILD-SHIP SCHEDULE

A build-ship schedule is a schedule of the ship date for each sales order in backlog and reservations. It is used by manufacturing to schedule production and by marketing to keep customers and sales representatives apprised of when sales orders are scheduled for shipment.

Build-Ship Schedule Date _____			
Ship Date	Sales Order	Quantity	Model

FIGURE 16-13   Build-ship schedule

TRAVELING REQUISITION

The traveling requisition is used in lieu of the purchase order form for repetitive purchases of parts and material for production. It saves clerical time.

Traveling Requisition				Description:		Part # :
Vendor:		Vendor:		Vendor:		Vendor:
Requisition Date	Quantity	P.O. #	P. O. Date	Vendor	Required Receipt Date	

FIGURE 16-14   Traveling requisition

WORK ORDER LOG

The work order log is a sequentially ascending number log of all work order numbers issued for a specific part number. It serves as an on-order record for work orders and as an audit trail for closed or completed work orders.

Work Order Log				Description:	Part # :
Lot	Quantity	Cut Date	Date Due	Complete Date	

FIGURE 16-15   Work order log

SHORT SHEET

The short sheet is a list of shortages used for expediting.

Date _____				Short Sheet　　　　　　　　Sheet ___ of ___
Part #	Quantity	Work Order	M A P	

FIGURE 16-16　　Short sheet

INVENTORY RECORD

The inventory record, sometimes called the perpetual inventory, records all receipts and withdrawals and the balance on hand of each active part number. The receipt identification number, usually a purchase order or completed work order number, is posted in the receipt column. An entry in the receipt column connotes a receipt. The withdrawal identification number, usually a work order number, is posted in the withdrawal column. An entry in the withdrawal column connotes a withdrawal.

Inventory Record					Description				Part # :
Date	Quantity	Receipt	With-drawal	On Hand Balance	Date	Quantity	Receipt	With-drawal	On Hand Balance

FIGURE 16-17   Inventory record

ON-ORDER RECORD

The on-order record lists all purchase orders issued for the part number
covered, noting receipts and the balance due on each open order. It is used
in the material requirements planning process and is an audit trail used
in expediting shortages.

On Order Record							Description:	Part #:
P.O. # Vendor	P.O. Date	Quantity	Required Delivery	Date Rec'd	Quantity Received	Balance Due		

FIGURE 16-18   On-order record

STOCK REQUISITION LOG

The stock requisition log is a log of withdrawals from the stockroom. It is used in a start-up situation with infrequent stockroom withdrawals and no stockroom clerk. It serves the same purpose as the stock requisition form.

Part #	Quantity	Used For		Cost		Post	
		Product	Reason	Each	Extended	Cost	Inventory

Stock Requisition Log Sheet___ of ___

FIGURE 16-19   Stock requisition log

STOCK TRANSFER LOG

The stock transfer log is a log of all individual transfers between work orders or between different inventory categories or classifications not covered by stock requisitions. It serves the same function as the stock transfer form. It is used in a start-up situation if there is no separate production function.

Part #	Quantity	Transfer		Cost		Post	
		From	To	Each	Extended	Cost	Inventory

Stock Transfer Log — Sheet ___ of ___

FIGURE 16-20   Stock transfer log

STOCK REQUISITION FORM

The stock requisition form records an individual withdrawal from the stockroom. It is the audit trail for the material or parts used in manufactured-part or assembly work orders.

Stock Requisition		
Qty:	Part # :	Work Order #
Date Filled:	Requisitioned By:	Filled By:

FIGURE 16-21   Stock requisition form

STOCK TRANSFER FORM

The stock transfer form records a transfer from one work order to another work order or from one inventory category to another inventory category. It is an audit trail for inventory transferred from one inventory classification to another inventory classification.

Stock Transfer			
Qty	Part # :	Date	By:
From:		To:	

FIGURE 16-22   Stock transfer form

TIME RECORD LOG

The time record log is a log of the time spent by each employee. It is used in a start-up situation with relatively few employees.

		Time Record Log			
Name _____				Sheet ___ of ___	
Date	Hours	Work Order #	Date	Hours	Work Order #

FIGURE 16-23   Time record log

QUOTATION

A quotation, sometimes called a bid or a proposal, is an offer to sell at a specified price and terms that is valid for a finite period of time.

Quantity	Part #	Description	Price	Extension

Quotation

Date _____

To:

Reference:

Total

F.O.B. _____

Terms _____

Valid Until _____

By _____

FIGURE 16-24   Quotation

SALES ORDER

A sales order, sometimes called an acknowledgement, is a response to or an acceptance of a customer purchase order.

```
┌──────────────────────────────────────────────────────────────────┐
│                         SALES ORDER                                │
│                                                                    │
│           Sales Order Number _____   Date _____        │
│                                                                    │
│          Customer P.O. Number _____   Date _____       │
│                                                                    │
│       Sold to:                    Ship to:                         │
│                                                                    │
│                                                                    │
│                                                                    │
├─────────┬────────┬──────────────────────┬─────────┬───────────────┤
│Quantity │ Part # │    Description        │  Price  │  Extension    │
│         │        │                       │         │               │
│         │        │                       │         │               │
│         │        │                       │         │               │
│         │        │                       │         │               │
│         │        │                       │         │               │
│         │        │                       ├─────────┴──── Total ──── │
│        F.O.B. ───────────────────────    │                         │
│        Terms: ───────────────────────    │                         │
│       Ship Via: ─────────────────────    │                         │
│       Delivery: ─────────────────────    │   By ─────────────────  │
└──────────────────────────────────────────┴─────────────────────────┘
```

FIGURE 16-25   Sales order

DEBIT-CREDIT MEMO

The debit-credit memo is used to record a dollar claim in favor of or against your company that is not expected to result in a cash payment. A debit memo is indicated by circling the word "debit." A credit memo is indicated by circling "credit."

```
                         DEBIT–CREDIT MEMO

  Debit-Credit Memo  # _____        Date: _____

  To:




  ┌─────────────────────────────────────────────┬─────────────┐
  │                   Item                        │   Amount    │
  ├─────────────────────────────────────────────┼─────────────┤
  │                                               │             │
  │                                               │             │
  │                                               │             │
  │                                               │             │
  │                          Debit-Credit Total   │             │
  ├─────────────────────────────────────────────┴─────────────┤
  │  Reference:                                                 │
  │                                                             │
  ├──────────────────────────────────┬──────────────────────── │
  │  Requested Disposition:           │                         │
  │                                   │                         │
  │                                   │   By_____    │
  └───────────────────────────────────┴─────────────────────── ┘
```

FIGURE 16-26   Debit-credit memo

DEBIT-CREDIT MEMO LOG

The debit-credit memo log is a sequentially ascending number log of all issued debit or credit memo numbers. An entry in the debit memo # column connotes a debit memo. An entry in the credit memo # column connotes a credit memo. It is an audit trail.

DEBIT-CREDIT MEMO LOG				
Debit Memo #	Credit Memo #	Date	Issued To	Description

FIGURE 16-27   Debit-credit memo log

VARIANCE REPORT

The variance report records variance from standard cost or hours. It is a managment tool that provides data on favorable or unfavorable variance trends.

	Jan	Feb	Mar	Apr	May	Jun	Jul	Aug	Sep	Oct	Nov	Dec
Actual												
Standard												
Variance												

Variance Report   Date _____

POSITIVE: 15% 10% 5% 0

NEGATIVE: 5% 10% 15%

Goal — — — —
Actual _____

FIGURE 16-28 Variance report

REPAIR-EXCHANGE WORK ORDER

The repair-exchange order covers the repair of a repair-exchange item. It is an audit trail.

REPAIR-EXCHANGE WORK ORDER				R-E W.O. # _____ Date _____
Part #	Rev.	Serial #		Description
Reference #		Received From:		Representative
Scope				
Disposition				
Repaired By:	Date:	Labor:	Material:	Total:

FIGURE 16-29   Repair-exchange work order

REPAIR-EXCHANGE WORK ORDER LOG

The repair-exchange work order log is a sequentially ascending number log of all issued repair-exchange work orders. It is used to avoid assigning the same number to two or more work orders. It is also an audit trail.

REPAIR-EXCHANGE WORK ORDER LOG							
R-E W.O. #	Date	Part #	Rev.	Serial #	Description	Customer	Service Representative

FIGURE 16-30   Repair-exchange work order log

SERIAL NUMBER LOG

The serial number log is a sequentially ascending number log of all issued serial numbers for a given part number. It is an audit trail to track the location of serial-numbered items.

SERIAL NUMBER LOG					Part # _____			
Serial #	Rev.	Parent Part #	Parent Serial #	Parent Rev.	Sales Order #	Date Shipped	Customer	

FIGURE 16-31   Serial number log

NOTICE OF REJECTION

The notice of rejection is a record of the reason for a rejection and the disposition of the discrepent parts or material.

Notice of Rejection				
Part # :	Description:	Vendor:		P. O. # :
Quantity:	Receiving Ticket # :	Rejected By:	Approved:	Date:
Reason for Rejection:				

Disposition	Approvals	Date
☐ Return to Vendor		
☐ Rework		
☐ Sort		
☐ Use as Is		

FIGURE 16-32   Notice of rejection

STOCK REQUIREMENT

The stock requirement serves as a purchase requisition and is used with the order-point material requirements planning system. It is usually attached to the minimum reorder quantity bag to trigger a procurement when the minimum reorder quantity is reached.

Stock Requirement			
Part # :		Description:	
Date	Quantity	P. O. #	Date Received

FIGURE 16-33   Stock requirement

RECEIVING TICKET

The receiving ticket is a record of an individual receipt of parts or material against an open purchase order.

Receiving Ticket	
Vendor Count:	Our Count:
Part # :	P. O. # :
Date Received:	By:
Date to Stock:	By:

FIGURE 16-34   Receiving ticket

ADVANCE NOTICE OF ENGINEERING CHANGE STAMP

The advance notice of engineering change is a rubber stamp affixed to a document, annotated to indicate that an engineering change has been made to the document.

Advance Notice of Engineering Change		
Document:		
Effectivity:		
By:	Date:	ECO #

FIGURE 16-35   Advance notice of engineering change stamp

SPECIAL-JOB STAMP

The special-job stamp is affixed to standard documents modified for the requirements of a special job. The special-job number is the sales order number. The special-job document number is the special-job number followed by a sequentially ascending number. The special-job bill of material serves as the special-job part number register.

Special Job	
S. O./Job	Part #
Date	By

FIGURE 16-36   Special-job stamp

TIME RECORD STAMP

The time record stamp is affixed to manufactured-part or assembly work orders. It is a log of time various operators have expended on the work order. It can be applied to any document for which time must be recorded.

Time Record			
Operator	Time On	Time Off	Hours

FIGURE 16-37   Time record stamp

WORK ORDER STAMP

The work order stamp is affixed to a production route sheet or an engineering drawing to convert the document to a manufactured-part work order or to a bill of material to create an assembly work order.

Work Order		
Lot #	Quantity:	Due:

FIGURE 16-38   Work order stamp

STOCK TRANSFER STAMP

The stock transfer stamp is affixed to manufactured-part or assembly work orders and notes transfers to another work order or to stock. It serves the same function as the stock transfer log and the stock transfer form.

Stock Transfer			
Qty	Transfer To	Date	By

FIGURE 16-39   Stock transfer stamp

ACCOUNT DISTRIBUTION STAMP

The account distribution stamp is affixed to vendor invoices and records distribution of invoice charges to appropriate accounts to provide an audit trail.

Account #	$
O. K. to pay:	Date:
Check #	Check Date:

FIGURE 16-40   Account distribution stamp

INDEX